BABYSITTERS ARE CHEAPER THAN DIVORCES

AND OTHER LESSONS I HOPE I HAVE PASSED DOWN TO MY CHILDREN

BY MARK D. OGLETREE, PH.D.

Produced with help from Hansen Book Consulting (HansenBookConsulting.com).

First Edition: February 2022

ISBN: 9798492664329

TABLE OF CONTENTS

INTRODUCTION

I am a blessed man. I really am. First, I am madly in love with my wife, Janie. We have been married for 38 years and counting. I still find myself looking at her and realizing how incredibly blessed my life is. Second, I have wonderful children whom I enjoy spending time with, laughing with, and learning from. Being a parent has been one of the great highlights of my life. Third, my grandchildren have been the greatest surprise of my life. When I married Janie back in the mid-1980s, I never even thought about the concept of grandchildren. In fact, I never realized how much I would love being a grandparent. Forth, I am grateful for my faith that is centered on our Lord, Jesus Christ. I see life through the lens of my family and my faith. Finally, I am blessed with an incredible double profession as a university professor, where I am privileged to interact with college students every day, and as a marriage and family therapist, where I am trusted to help people navigate their way through the most difficult challenges they have in life.

I feel that Janie and I have been good parents for the most part. Not that we are better than other parents are, but we certainly have desired to be good parents, and we have spent a significant portion of our lives studying what good parents do.

Early in our parenting journey, we realized that we needed some additional help. We read books, talked with experts, and attended workshops and seminars on parenting. One of our main priorities was to raise a good, healthy family. We hoped that our children would be strong contributors to society; we hoped they would become leaders, and we wanted them to raise good families as well. We have not been perfect in this endeavor, but it is where we have spent most of our energy.

I need to be clear that we are not a perfect family—in fact, not even close. As parents, we make mistakes daily, and our children have followed our example with their own faults and shortcomings. However, what I love most about our children is that they are hardworking, resilient, faith-filled, happy, funny, and devoted now to their own families.

The origins of this book come from two places. First, as our children were leaving the nest—heading off to college, on missions for our Church, or into marriage—like most parents, we often found ourselves wondering, "Did we teach them that principle?", "Did we ever cover that?", or "How will they know how to do that?" I came to realize that not everything children need to know could be covered in 18 years. Furthermore, I also recognize that many of the lessons they need to understand will have to be learned on their own. Nevertheless, I wanted to make my own instruction manual for my children, based on the idea that we may have never discussed some important material for the exam of life! Having read Jackson Brown's *Life's Little Instruction Book* many years ago, I wanted to make a customized instruction booklet for my own children, that also could be shared with others.

Secondly, our children may have forgotten some of the things that we *did* teach them, or at least, that I *thought* we had taught them. For example, several years ago our family was on a vacation. As part of our travels, we stayed the night at the home of one of our friends in Arizona. The next morning, as we were pulling out of their driveway to head home, I asked my adult children—some were married, and some were not—if they had cleaned the room they had just slept in and if they had made the room look better than they found it. Several of them answered that they had not. I stopped the car, pulled back into the driveway, and had my *adult* children go back into our friend's home and get cleaning.

Now, here is why I feel so passionate about leaving things better than you found them. Throughout our married years, we occasionally have had friends and family come visit our home and stay with us. I was surprised how many people left our house a complete mess when they drove away. Some did not even try to clean up after themselves. For that reason, and many others, this aspect of guest etiquette became a passion of mine, and I was constantly drilling that concept into our children's heads when we were guests in other people's homes. I wanted our children to adhere to the principle that we should always leave places better than we found them. I taught our children that practicing such a principle might be the only way we get invited back! However, on this early morning in Arizona, I began to question myself. Did I really teach this principle? Did Janie? Or did I just think we did? Were my children listening when we taught it? Did they accept that teaching, or did they think it was ridiculous?

Over time, as I have watched my adult children start their marriages and then ultimately began raising children of their own, I have often asked myself, "Didn't we cover that topic when they were growing up?" Then I have wondered, "Were they not listening, or did we not teach the principle plainly?" To be clear, I have learned that our children will not agree with or want to teach their children everything we taught them. However, there are some basic principles that every adult needs to understand and practice.

Therefore, with the premise that (1) my wife and I may have forgotten to teach our children several things, (2) our children may not have listened, and (3) they may have forgotten, I present this helpful little instruction manual to you and to my children. I have affectionately titled it, *"Babysitters Are Cheaper Than Divorces—And Other Lessons I Hope I Have Passed Down to My Children."* This book has been in the process of development for many years. Occasionally, when I would think of something that we should have taught our children or that they may have forgotten, I would record the lesson. Over the course of the past ten years, my list grew longer and longer. Finally, about one year ago, I realized that I had enough material to make a book. I have added pictures and some occasional stories to give the book some "life."

This book is designed so that you can turn to any topic that you are interested in and read about it. The topics are short and concise—meaning that many of the lessons are covered on one page and some on two pages, but no more than that. If you are a parent or grandparent, I would admonish you to keep teaching and influencing your posterity! Parenting is the most difficult endeavor in life, but also the most rewarding! On the other hand, grandparenting can be just plain fun and rewarding! If you are not married or have a family, I invite you to begin recording some of your own life lessons. You never know who you may share them with later in life!

Janie, the love of my life! Thirty-six years of marriage, eight children, and twenty grandchildren. Do you think we can go another thirty-six?

BARGAINS

"Use it up, wear it out, make it do, or do without."
~ Boyd K. Packer[1]

Years ago, I took several of my children to a Dallas Mavericks game in the newly constructed American Airlines Center. We did not have much money in those days, but I had been given a good tip by a neighbor that I could get a great deal on tickets from the scalpers. I received another tip that if I waited until after the opening game tip off, the tickets would be drastically cheaper. Therefore, not long after the game had started, I approached a scalper. We haggled a bit over the cost, and I ended up getting myself and three of my teenagers in the arena for $40. The scalper was not too thrilled, but we were excited.

After each quarter of the game, we moved down to seats closer to courtside. It was a lopsided game—the Mavericks were killing the opponent—so fans began leaving the game early. By the fourth quarter, my children and I were sitting on the front row in courtside seats! I remember how accomplished (or lucky) I felt to be eating the popcorn and peanuts that the previous fans had left while I read the $10 program that was lying under a chair. It was a-once in-a-lifetime opportunity to be with my children in that setting—a real bargain!

A few years before our Dallas Mavericks experience, our family lived in Mesa, Arizona. In those days, grocery stores would often double or triple the worth of their coupons. For example, there were coupons for one dollar off a box of cereal. If the grocery store chain doubled—or sometimes tripled their coupons—then you could literally walk out of the grocery store with a box of cereal for 50 cents. Or, better yet, four boxes of cereal for a dollar. Sometimes you were actually being paid by the store to haul things out to your car. For my wife, this became her sport. In fact, if they would have had "couponing" as an extracurricular activity at her high school, she could have lettered in it. So, for several years, a couple of evenings a week, we would load our children into our minivan like a bunch of hunters heading out on a safari. Where were we going? To newspaper recycling bins across town. My wife and several of our children would literally lower themselves into the newspaper dumpster and go through the Sunday advertisements from the local paper and pull out all the coupons. My job was to be on the lookout for any suspicious activity, but the only thing suspicious was a mother and her five children, diving in dumpsters.

I know, some of you are relating this experience to the Nicolas Cage scene in the movie, *Raising Arizona*, in which Cage's character, "H.I. 'Hi' McDonnough," steals a bundle of Huggies diapers, at gunpoint, from a convenience store. I promise that this was nothing like that! Members of the community were simply donating their unwanted newspaper to the recycling program.

After we had hit up several recycling bins, we would go home, and my wife would spend hours cutting out and organizing her coupons. Then she was finally off to her favorite grocery store, returning home with 75 tubes of toothpaste that she got for 50 cents or a crate of dental floss for $1.25. I say again—what a bargain

Suggestions:

- Do not be shy about using coupons and groupons.

- Find deals at yard sales and garage sales. I knew a relatively wealthy family who, each year, purchased their entire families' Christmas at yard sales.

- Discover the power of purchasing used things—especially things that your children, or the neighbors, will probably destroy anyway. Swing sets, weightlifting equipment, trampolines, bikes, camping gear, water and snow skiing accessories, and basketball hoops can be purchased on websites or through classified ads where used merchandise is sold.

- Do not ever be afraid to negotiate the price on something that another person is selling. If you have a fist full of cash to offer, people will often take less than their asking price.

- Never pay full price for a car.

- If it makes sense, purchase items in bulk.

 *More on bargains*

BEST HEALTH PRACTICES

"Health is certainly more valuable than money,
because it is by health that money is procured…"
~ Samuel Johnson[2]

As a kid, I do not remember my parents playing much with us outdoors. Although my dad always coached our teams, that was about the extent of their outdoor involvement. However, I remember that I used to see families occasionally playing together in their yards or driveways. I recall even seeing some families spending time on the tennis courts, golf courses, or jogging trails. I hoped that one day I would be able to participate in outdoor activities with my own children.

Good health should be a most-valued commodity. Janie and I have tried to stay in good physical shape so that we could enjoy time with our children during their adolescent and adult years. We have always belonged to a health club as a family so that we can exercise together. I am grateful that I can jog with my children and that we can play racquetball and pickle ball together. I am also happy that we can go on long mountain hikes and ski together. I attribute this blessing to trying to take good care of my body. I have not been perfect in this endeavor, but I am grateful for what my health allows me to do with my children and grandchildren.

Suggestions:

- Buy a new showerhead about every two years. A good massage showerhead can cure a multitude of ailments. I have learned that you can shave, brush your teeth, and do about twelve other things while in the shower. Stay in that shower as long as you can.

- Engage in regular cardiovascular exercise.

- Take vitamins daily.

- Drink smoothies.

- Ride bicycles—it's a great form of exercise, and easy on the knees and ankles.

- Lift weights.

- As Jackson Brown suggested, "Never open the refrigerator when you're bored."[3]

- Join a health club and take advantage of their hot tub and steam room.

- Visit your family doctor each year for a full physical and insist the same for your spouse and children. If you get significantly hurt, go to the doctor. Do not assume the problem will just go away. My father died at a young age, partly because he refused to go to the doctor when he had symptoms telling him that he should have. Also, visit the dentist every six months to a year.

- Invest in a good bed—you will spend half of your life on it. Unbelievably, you will spend more time in your life sleeping than working, socializing, engaging in recreation, and exercising. Experts estimate that the average American will spend 26 years sleeping, and 7 years trying to go to sleep.[4] Since such a large portion of your life will be spent in bed, I recommend that you invest in a nice mattress.

 *More on best health practices*

BEST FAMILY PRACTICES

"Home: The Place to Save Society."
~ Spencer W. Kimball[5]

Many years ago, I was jumping on our trampoline with some of our children. My three-year old daughter, Bethany, was just learning to count. With the recent birth of our twin daughters, the number of children in our family was up to five. While jumping on the trampoline, Bethany said to me, "Dad, just think, if we could get just two more kids, we could be Snow White and the Seven Dwarfs." That was hilarious to me. Her little three-year-old mind was cranking. I immediately thought that my wife could probably be Snow White in my little daughter's story, but I would probably be cast as one of the seven dwarfs—probably Grumpy or Dopey. This experience, as well as many others, made we wish I had recorded so many of the funny things that my children said.

Suggestions:

- Take many photographs and videos of your family. Yes, take tons of pictures and share them often. Save your digital photos on an external hard drive, and keep it somewhere other than your home.

- Be consistent in writing down the humorous things that your children say. Keep these expressions in a journal or scrapbook.

- Consider painting the inside and outside of your home every four to five years and rearrange the furniture in your home occasionally.

- Play music loud enough in your home that everyone can dance while doing their chores! Every mom and dad should be a dancing fool, if for no other reason than just to embarrass their children. Begin each day with good music playing throughout your home.

- Always have good food in your home. Food will keep your children close by. Food will also keep your children's friends within a close proximity—definitely a double-edged sword!

- Create a place in your home where your family can interact, talk, and laugh without any interruptions. Have a special place where love can be shared and where values can be taught.

- Create a culture of fun and laughter in your home. If you do not, your children may go to someone else's home to find fun and humor.

BEST PREPAREDNESS PRACTICES

"The time to repair the roof is when the sun is shining."
~ John F. Kennedy[6]

At the age of sixteen, I was driving with two of my best friends across the West Texas Desert at 2:00 in the morning. We were on our way to a camping trip in the Rocky Mountains. I was at the wheel and glanced at the gas gauge. I recognized that I had not been paying close attention to our fuel supply. We were on empty, and I knew that the nearest gas station would not be for a hundred miles. I woke one of my friends up and explained our predicament. He said, "No big deal." Then he leaned toward the dashboard and flipped a switch. I said, "What did you just do?" He explained that his van had two gas tanks, and that he had just changed the fuel supply to the reserve tank. I remember thinking how cool that was, but I also learned a great lesson on being prepared.

On another occasion, we were out with a group of teenagers, and someone in our group asked, "Does anyone have a Band-Aid?" My same friend said, "I do," and then he pulled a Band-Aid out of his wallet. Unfortunately, in my life, I have not always been so prepared. However, it is never too late to learn the lessons that will bless our lives and the lives of others.

Suggestions:

- Create a killer "first-aid" kit with your family.

- Learn CPR and basic first-aid skills.

- Build and maintain a three-month supply of food and water in your home (if you lack storage space, you can store a supply of water and canned goods underneath every bed in your home).

- Have an emergency fund so that you can live comfortably for three to six months. Make sure that some of this fund is in cash.

- Develop an emergency home exit plan for your family in case of a fire or disaster. Identify a meeting place for if your family has to get out of your home quickly.

- If you have more than one level on your home, own escape ladders that can hang down from the second-story windows.

- It is not a bad idea to keep fire extinguishers in your home, cars, and recreational vehicles.

- Make a video recording of your home, clothing, furniture, appliances, electronics, tools, and other valuables. This practice could be most helpful for insurance purposes.

- Make sure smoke detectors and CO2 detectors are installed in your home and in the proper places. Check the batteries in these devices often.

- Make sure the spare tire in your car has air in it. I learned this lesson the hard way.

- Make sure you have spare keys for your cars and your home.

- Own a Coleman camp stove and/or a Jetboil. These are essential items for camping and can be used in case of an emergency.

- Create a 72-hour emergency kit for every member of your family.

- Keep an empty gas can and a first-aid kit in the trunk of your car.

- Own a Swiss army knife.

- Ensure that every member of your family has a flashlight and keep a supply of fresh batteries on hand. It is best to keep a flashlight in each room of the house.

- Invest in a generator, a propane heater, and a water filter. If you want to take this a step further, you can have your home wired to run off a generator.

- Store some extra fuel in a safe place.

- Cut down your own firewood.

- Always have duct tape close by.

More on best preparedness practices:
Stinky Island and winter drives

BIRTHDAYS

"Happy birthday! May your Facebook wall be filled with messages from people you never talk to."
~ From a Birthday Card

I grew up in a family that certainly recognized your birthday. I definitely remember getting gifts and having parties. When I became older, our family usually went out to dinner, and I received some age-appropriate gifts—like clothes. However, when I married Janie, I recognized that her family celebrated birthdays on an entirely different level. First, each meal of the day was a customized experience—your favorite breakfast, your favorite restaurant for lunch, and, of course, your favorite dinner. On your birthday, there was a special red plate for you at the dinner table, and everyone treated you like a rock star.

When Janie and I had our own children, we added a few more elements to the birthday celebration. Most often, that evening, we went around the room, taking turns saying kind and positive things about the birthday boy or girl. The air in the room was filled with praise, compliments, and love. This is a practice that continues today and has been passed down to the next generation. A birthday celebration is an opportunity to tell someone how much they mean to us and how boring life would be without them! When it comes to birthdays, I say, "Go big or go home."

Suggestions:

- A birthday is a celebration of a loved one's life—not merely a chance to eat cake and ice cream.

- Make birthdays big celebrations in your family. They are opportunities to show a child or spouse how important they are in the world, community, neighborhood, and in your family.

- When giving birthday gifts, try to pay special attention to what the "birthday person" wants or needs. When I am with family members, I try to notice what they "borrow" from me or what they tell me they need. When visiting their homes, I often think, "What could this person use that would make their day?"

- A fun birthday tradition is to have everyone give a compliment or share how the birthday person has positively influenced his or her life.

- Adult children, when your parents are older, do the same thing for them. Make your parents' birthday celebrations a big deal—and do not assume someone else is going to do it.

- Always call parents, siblings, grandparents, and in-laws on their birthday or send them a nice note or card. Wish people happy birthday on social media platforms.

- Recognize the birthdays of other people in your life, outside of your family, such as co-workers, neighbors, church members, friends, and others. Send them a card, a text, or an email. People love to be remembered on their birthday.

- When you receive birthday gifts, or any gifts for that matter from someone else, never give those gifts back to the giver. Better yet, never say to the giver, "I don't really need this. Why don't you keep it?" When someone gives you a gift, whether you like it or not, accept the gift with love and respect. I am aware of an individual who, if they receive a gift that they do not like, they hand it right back to the giver.

 *More birthday stories*

BORROWING STUFF

"Infringe upon the rights of no one. Borrow no tool but what you will return according to promise.
~ Brigham Young[7]

I will never forget the time that we loaned a brand-new DVD to one of our friends. They never mentioned anything about giving it back. In fact, three weeks passed, and they still had not returned the DVD, so we sent one of our children over to their home to retrieve it. One of our daughters drove over to their home, knocked on the door, and asked for the DVD. The neighbor said, "Oh, we're sorry. We do not have it anymore. We loaned it to another neighbor." So our daughter asked the next obvious question, "What neighbor?" Our friend said, "I don't remember." Our daughter then inquired, "So, how could we get our DVD back?" The neighbor responded, "I don't know.... I'm really sorry about that?" And that was it. No offering to track the DVD down, nor was there an offering to purchase a new DVD to replace the one they lost. The neighbor essentially was saying, "Thanks for the DVD. When we were done watching it, we just flushed it down the toilet. We hope you're okay with that."

A few years earlier, another neighbor watched our home and our dogs for us while we were on vacation. When we arrived home, many of our video cassettes were gone. A few days later, the neighbor came to our front door and said, "Here are some of your videos. I brought them home to watch while you were on vacation." I said, "Thank you for bringing them back. But do you know where the covers are for the videos?" The neighbor said, "Oh, sorry, I guess we lost them."

My favorite was the neighbor who borrowed some of our camping equipment. After several weeks, as usual, we had to drive to our neighbor's house to track down our equipment they had borrowed. When I knocked on their door and asked for our things, the neighbor seemed annoyed that I wanted our stuff back. I was quite confused about that. I was not trying to be a jerk, but we were going camping and needed our stuff! We did them a favor and then were in trouble for it! Perhaps it would be easier, and more convenient, to purchase the equipment that you need rather than borrow it from a neighbor or family member and never return it.

Suggestions:

- A wise man once recommended that we should only lend those things to others that we never want to see again. Certainly, do not ever lend out your "favorite" things.

- Here is a good rule of thumb from Jackson Brown when it comes to borrowing: "If you borrow something more than twice, buy one for yourself."[8]

Yes, if you have to borrow something quite often, then it is time to buy one for yourself.

- When loaning things out to others, recognize that you may have to go track those things down a few weeks later. Why not ask the borrower, "So, when will you be bringing this back?" After all, it is your stuff!

- When borrowing things from others, always return those things as soon as possible. We have had people borrow things from us who have still never returned them. This makes me wonder if I have done the same!

- When borrowing something from others, return the item better condition than you found it. For instance, if you borrow a person's truck, clean it and fill it with gas before you give it back.

- If you borrow something from someone and damage it, buy the lender a new replacement. Here is my rule: *if you broke it, you bought it.*

- Do not shy away from buying things rather than borrowing them. Sometimes it is easier to purchase the item you need rather than put a strain on the relationship by borrowing something and breaking it or forgetting to return the item.

- Do not ever borrow something from someone that you could not replace. For example, if you borrow someone's car, could you replace it if you wrecked it? If not, then do not borrow it!

- I recommend that you do not ever ask to borrow brand-new or sentimental items from others. Do not ever borrow something from someone that is so new they have never used it!

- Do not ever borrow money from friends or, if possible, from family.

More on borrowing stuff

BOUNDARIES FOR ADULT CHILDREN AND PARENTS/IN-LAWS

"Good fences make good neighbors."
~Robert Frost[9]

I believe the key to parent and adult-children relationships is the principle of reciprocity. This means that the relationship must be mutually beneficial. When children are young, the relationship between parent and child is often one sided. For example, parents bless, serve, and help their children, but children do very little for their parents. However, as children grow up, they can, and should, do more for their parents. In fact, once children become adults, the benefits, service, and care should be bi-directional—both parties should bless, help, and serve each other. Finally, when parents become senior citizens, their children should do more for them—not less.

A friend of mine made the following observation. He told me about the relationship he had with his wife's parents. He said, "When we were younger, it seemed there were many occasions when Lisa's parents did nice things for us. If we were in a financial pinch, they were there to help us out. If we had to travel a long distance to visit them for Christmas, they were able to donate some money for the trip. When we lived closer to each other, if we needed a tool, they had one we could borrow. However, as her parents became older, the roles reversed somewhat. We were able to help more financially; we were finally in a position where we could pay for meals, hotels, travel, and even had tools they could borrow." And just like my friends' in-laws seemed to watch over them when they were a young married couple, now he and his wife were watching over her parents as they became senior citizens. This, I believe, is a great example of how reciprocity works.

Suggestions:

- Discuss with your spouse the role that you hope your parents and in-laws will have in your marriage and family life. For example, when having a baby, discuss with your parents and in-laws the role you would like them to take in helping you.

- Be somewhat guarded in what you communicate to your parents and in-laws. They do not need to know everything. Avoid telling your parents the "nitty-gritty" details about your marriage or your children. Long after the issues have subsided, your parents or in-laws may still believe those issues are continuing.

- Resist the temptation to revert to the role of a child when you are around your parents.

- Do not "overuse" your parents to babysit your children.

- When you visit your in-laws or parents, always pick up their home before you leave. Make their house look like it did before you arrived. Do not let your children bounce or climb all over their furniture, write on their walls, or rub chocolate all over the television screen (hypothetically speaking).

- When your children break things at their grandparent's home, you should offer to pay for the repair or purchase a new item for them. Do not just walk away or ignore the fact that your child just shattered your parents' front window. In addition, do not assume a magic genie will ultimately show up and fix it.

Breaking Things

BOUNDARIES FOR PARENTS OF ADULT CHILDREN—GRANDPARENTS

"Dr. Mother-in-law, never tell me how to handle my children. I am living with one of yours and they need a lot of improvement."
~ *Author Unknown*

A friend of mine told me the following. He said that when he was a young father, his in-laws would visit often. Once he was feeding his baby daughter some lunch as she sat in her highchair. His baby did not like what she was being fed, and so she spit the food out. Immediately, his mother-in-law said, "What are you going to do to your daughter for spitting out her food?" My friend said, "I don't know, probably nothing—she's a baby." Then his mother-in-law said, "Well, we did not tolerate that behavior in our home. If our child did that, we would have spanked her." My friend then kindly replied, "Well, we don't want to do that—we don't necessarily want to do everything you all did as parents. In fact, you will probably find over the years that we may raise our children a little differently than you all did." It was certainly a tense moment, but a young father was putting a healthy boundary in place. His in-laws were not going to dictate how they raised their children. Good for him.

Suggestions:

- Grandparents, here is your most important role: Just love your grandchildren and have fun with them! Make some memories with them that they will always treasure. Make sure you have a healthy, positive relationship with each grandchild.

- Establish some rules in your home so that when your adult children and their children (your grandchildren) visit, they know the rules and boundaries.

- Do not give your adult children advice unless they ask for it (unless you write a book like this—that is legal).

- Do not boss your grandchildren around or discipline them. Grandparents do not make parenting decisions. Go to the parents for discipline issues.

- Do not expect your children to parent the same way you did. Try to enforce the same rules and standards with your grandchildren that their parents have for them. For example, if parents have set a curfew for their teenagers to be home by 11:30 p.m., do not undermine the parents by saying something like, "That's a stupid rule, you should be able to stay out as long as you would like." If you do that, your adult children will begin to feel that you are wearing out your welcome.

- Do not give your grandchildren food or candy that their parents would not approve of or even let them play video games or watch movies that their parents would not support.

- Never assume that you have free reign to barge into your adult children's homes anytime you want to. Always ask if they are home and if it is okay to come for a visit. Respect their time and their schedule.

- Grandparents have no right or input when it comes to naming grandchildren. Resist the temptation to speak out when you hear that your child is going to name their baby something that you would have never named them.

- Teach your grandchildren about their heritage. Tell them stories about your life. Share with them life lessons that they can pass down to the next generation.

- Do not simply help your adult children in the manner that *you* think they need help. Always ask, "What would you like us to do?" and then go and do that! If you are showing up to their home and cleaning their house when they were hoping you would take the children to a park and play with them, they will be frustrated with you.

- When it comes to giving your grandchildren gifts for birthdays and Christmas, consider providing them with "experiences" instead of material possessions. For example, take them on a trip or some kind of outing, instead of purchasing a gift for them that they may never use or that will be broken by the next day.

With our grandchildren on the beach in California.

BUILDING RELATIONSHIPS

"Relationships include taking time to be with each other. They are also about sensing the other person's unique hopes and wishes... Relationships are not built while running a stopwatch. They grow when people take time to be together."
~ *Dr. Wallace H. Goddard*[10]

My father-in-law was the master of relationships. He served people without ever expecting anything in return. Whenever in his presence, he made sure he built you up and complimented you. If something good happened to you, he was the first to call to congratulate you or one of your children. I never left his presence where I did not feel like a better person. In fact, to be in his company was to be healed, strengthened, and renewed. I have always hoped that I could be like that for my own family.

I remember when Janie had our second baby, our son, Brandon. It was a very difficult delivery, and she had many complications afterwards. She came closer to death than I ever wanted to imagine. During one of these difficult days, my father-in-law called us on the phone in our hospital room. After talking to him for some time, he said, "So, how are you doing?"

Thankfully, I was able to say, "Janie is getting much better. She's getting stronger every day, and the baby is also doing well." As I continued to talk, he stopped me in my in my tracks. He said with more emphasis, "No, how are **YOU** doing?" —and he certainly emphasized the **YOU** part. Up to that point, the situation had been so intense that I really did not know how I was doing. No one had asked me that question during our difficult trials and challenges in the hospital. All of the emphasis had been on Janie and our baby son—as it should have been. But my father-in-law was thinking outside the box, inquiring how all of these challenges were affecting me. That was so kind of him. I gave him an appropriate response, but I also learned a great lesson. Sometimes the caretakers or those who are not hospitalized or injured can be easily forgotten during difficult times.

One of the things about my father-in-law that I will never forget was his consistency in phone calls. Over time, I realized that my day for the weekly phone call was Friday. I am a university professor, and typically, I do not teach classes on Fridays. Therefore, for many years, I received a phone call from him every Friday. When my father-in-law died, one of his sons spoke at his funeral. He said, "When I think of my dad, I think of this"—pulling out his cell phone. He then he began to weep and said, "I'm going to miss no longer receiving phone calls every Thursday from my dad. He was my best friend." That was a man who knew how to build and maintain relationships.

Suggestions:

- Make time to build relationships. Try not to give people the impression you are in a hurry. Do not look at your watch or the clock while you are interacting with others.

- Compliment people and be free with praise. Any idiot can be critical of others—it actually takes brains and talent to find the good in others. Complimenting builds relationships! A healthy practice is to give at least one daily compliment to the people you love the most and spend the most time with.

- Be positive and optimistic. Most people prefer not to associate with individuals who are negative and pessimistic. Always find the good in other people and in difficult situations. If you can do so, you will be an influence for good to those around you.

- When in discussions with others, ask them questions about their lives, their families, and their work. Listen attentively. Asking questions about others' lives shows that you are interested in them. Try to avoid the temptation to talk solely about yourself when in a conversation with someone else. Ask the questions and allow others to talk.

- Remember the things that are important to others—names, family members, events, hobbies, interests. Call people by name. Inquire about their family members by name.

- If you can master the art of being an attentive listener, and asking appropriate questions, people will be drawn to you because they will know that you care. When in conversations with others, do not be overly anxious to be a "topper" or a "one-upper." Gladly listen to people and believe that you can learn something from everyone.

- When in doubt about what to talk to people about, ask them about their families. Find out how their spouse, children, and grandchildren are doing. If they do not have immediate family, ask them about their work, school, or other interests.

- If you know someone who has a member of their family who is sick or has a disease, inquire about their sick family member often.

- Manage your technology—smart phones are relationship killers. You cannot build a relationship with someone while you are playing on your phone.

 *Steve Cook—Master of Relationships*

BUYING STUFF

"Most of the things we buy are wants.
We call them needs, but they're wants."
~ Dave Ramsey[11]

I will never forget the first time we purchased a minivan back in the early 1990s. We really did not have the money to buy the vehicle, but we thought we would visit a car dealership and at least look. With five small children, a minivan would have been the perfect remedy. Janie had just given birth to twin daughters, and we instantly outgrew our previous vehicle. The eager used-car salesman sprinted over to us and began his sales pitch before we could even look at the interior of the van. I explained to him several times that we were only there to look. Finally, he said, "What would it take to have your business and sell you this car today?" I said, "Do you really want to know?" He said, "Yes!" I said, "Okay, here's the deal. I am a full-time schoolteacher attending graduate school. We do not have much money; in fact, we owe people money. Therefore, if you want to sell me this van, here is what would be the requirements. First, you need to lower the asking price by several thousand dollars. Second, our monthly payment cannot be over $250 per month. Finally, you need to take my Subaru in for a trade, and I need you to give me a thousand dollars in cash." I thought my incredible request would get the salesman off my scent—especially when I told him I needed to walk off the lot with $1000 in cash. He said, "Okay, let me go talk to Tony." I assumed that Tony was his manager. Unbelievably, he came back a few minutes later and said, "You've got deal." Even as I write this today, I believe purchasing that minivan was a miracle.

Suggestions:

- Make it a practice to avoid purchasing items that you do not need. It is that simple, folks. Buy things you need, and do not buy stuff that you do not—even if it's "on sale."

- For purchases over $50-$100, always consult with your spouse.

- When purchasing cars, make sure you consult the *Kelly Blue Book*. Then, take the vehicles for a test drive—and that does not mean just around the block. You need to get that car out on the freeway and make sure the wheels do not pop off while you are going 70 miles per hour. You also want to be sure that car does not rattle and shake like the Space Shuttle reentering the atmosphere as you travel at freeway speed. Finally, always offer the seller less than they are asking. Haggling should take place over every car purchase. In fact, I know some people who do not mind haggling over produce at the grocery store.

- Before large purchases, consider "sleeping on it" before making the decision to buy a large-ticket item, such as a home or car. If you feel pressured to buy something immediately, I recommend walking away.

- Much of the sports and outdoor equipment that you need can be purchased from stores like "Play it Again Sports" or found in classified ads. Swing sets, trampolines, ski equipment and other sports equipment, and accessories for your boats or campers can all be purchased used instead of new.

- Never pay a contractor or a service provider until they have completed the job. This is another lesson we learned the hard way.

- When buying things, ask yourself questions like:

  - How bad to we need this item?

  - Will we want this item one year from now?

  - Could we purchase a cheaper version of this item?

  - After a good night's sleep, will I still want this item tomorrow?

 *A story about buying stuff*

CAREER

*"To find a career to which you are adapted by nature,
and then to work hard at it, is about as near to a formula for
success and happiness as the world provides.*
~ Mark Sullivan[12]

It was the mid-1970s, and my parents had just purchased a brand-new home in the suburbs of Houston, Texas. We moved into that home before the grass had been planted. I remember one day, shortly after we moved in, coming home from middle school and walking across the newly planted grass in the front yard. As I walked towards the side of the house, checking out our new lawn, a very old man came walking towards me. This man was part of the landscaping crew that was working on our yard. He was straining as he carried a wheelbarrow full of rocks, weeds, and debris. He had a cigarette hanging out of his mouth, and he looked like he had just escaped from working in a coal mine.

He said to me, "Son, did you learn anything at school today?" I said, "Yes sir." Then he said something I've never forgotten. He said, "Son, stay in school and receive all of the education you can get. If you do not, then you will end up like me. You will be 80 years old and working on a lawn crew." Talk about "scared straight." I have always remembered that lesson taught to me by that stranger. Who would have thought at that time, as a seventh grader in middle school that I would have ended up being a university professor? I promise—not me. Nevertheless, the words of that old man echoed in my ears at several critical junctures of my life.

Suggestions:

- Find a career that you can be passionate about—something that you love waking up for each day.

- Discover a career where you can utilize your natural talents, gifts, passions, and abilities.

- Obtain the fullest of formal education so that you can rise to the top of your career. That could mean graduate school. I know that there is always that individual in your community who is a millionaire and graduated only from high school. I have known that person everywhere where we have lived. Trust me: they are the exception rather than the rule. Education pays. The more education you have, the more money you will earn.

- Choose a career that is family friendly. You will want to make money and provide for your family—but if you are never home because of the rigors of your job, you could end up failing your family. Your career should help you create a lifestyle where you can have wonderful experiences with your family on a regular basis. Remember the wise words from church leader David O. McKay, who was actually quoting J. E. McCullough: "No other success can compensate for failure in the home."[13]

- Cultivate and develop strong personal relationships at your workplace. It will be where you spend most of your time.

- Be the first one to your office, but do not worry about being the last one to leave. You have loved ones waiting for you!

- Dress for success. Wear well-pressed shirts or dresses and polish your shoes regularly.

- Never close any doors. If someone wants to talk to you about a potential job or position, even though you are satisfied where you presently are, still listen and show interest.

- Continue to bolster and strengthen your knowledge and skills in your chosen profession. This will mean subscribing to journals and attending workshops and seminars to stay on the "cutting-edge." Also, read books specific to your career that will provide insight and information to you that will improve your professional trajectory and enable you to bless and strengthen those you work with.

- Take the time to decorate your office and make it comfortable. For most men, you will most likely spend more time in your office that anywhere else in life, so make it a home away from home. I have always enjoyed having a refrigerator in my office, a microwave, tons of food, good books, and music going on all day. Create an incredible "homey" environment at your office.

- Always have pictures of your family in your office: it will remind you and demonstrate to others where your greatest priority is.

- When you travel with your work, include your family when possible. Occasionally, bring your spouse and/or children to professional conferences!

Presenting a Paper at a Professional Conference in Orlando, Florida, and then having fun at Disneyworld the next day with Janie and the girls.

CARS

"If you think nobody cares if you are alive,
try missing a couple of car payments."
~ Earl Wilson[14]

When our oldest daughter left for college, we decided to drive her from Dallas to Southeastern Idaho and make a family vacation out of the journey. We were in our 15-passenger van, pulling a small trailer. Unfortunately, about 40 miles west of Albuquerque, our car overheated, and subsequently, the engine blew up. We did not know it at the time, but most of the pistons in the engine were shot. A friend in Albuquerque helped me replace the radiator hose, and then we continued our journey to Utah and then to Idaho. Yes, the van rode "rough," but it continued like a trooper.

We were able to get our daughter moved in and then drive the rest of the way home to Texas. We scheduled an appointment with our mechanic, and he went right to work on the engine. In short order, he broke the bad news to us: our entire engine needed to be rebuilt. When I told him what happened and how far we drove on that bad engine, he was in a state of complete disbelief. He said, "That van should have never been able to make that trip after Albuquerque." He kept saying, "That's impossible." We know that God was watching over us and that he allowed us to get home safely. That was the good news. The bad news was that for the money we spent repairing the van, we probably could have just purchased a new one!

Suggestions:

- Cars are not an investment; they are an expense. They lose their value the minute you drive them off the lot. Do not buy into the false notion that your car will be worth more after you drive it around for several years and shred it.

- Resist the temptation to buy a brand-new car. Purchasing good, certified used cars can provide you with a reliable car for a cheaper price.

- Find a good, honest mechanic, and be loyal to their establishment. Finding a mechanic you can trust is almost as valuable as finding the right doctor.

- Choose a reputable tire store and frequent them often. Get to know the staff and show them your loyalty. They will often help you get the best deal, and they will most likely repair your flat tires for free.

- Take pride in the appearance of your car. Wash your car at least once a month and keep the inside clean. Each time you park your car in your driveway or garage, take the garbage out of your car, as well as other items that can be stored in your home or apartment.

- Never let your gas tank fall below a quarter of a tank.

- Teach your children basic repairs, like how to change the oil, battery, air filter, and a flat tire.

- Do not be afraid to use YouTube videos to learn how to do some minor repairs on your car.

- Make sure you keep a small first aid kit, jumper cables, and a towrope in your cars.

- It never hurts to make friends with a neighbor or friend who knows how to fix cars. Everywhere we have lived, I have always had a friend I could ask about basic car repairs. Find that friend!

- Keep a spare key to your car in a magnetic box that you can hide somewhere on the exterior of your vehicle.

Posing with our favorite family vehicle—Big Red. We traveled across the country in this van several times, went camping, brought our children to college, and Janie drove them to school each day. I miss ole' Big Red.

 *My Children, My Car*

CELL PHONE ETIQUETTE

"Life is not confined to a four-inch screen."
~ Jose A. Teixeira[15]

Just recently, our family was in San Antonio, Texas, celebrating Christmas with our daughter Brittany, her husband Tyler, and their children. We went out for lunch on Christmas Eve. While waiting for our food, we were talking and enjoying each other's company. A family with several teenagers were sitting just across the aisle from us. I could not help but notice that each member of their family—the mother, father, and their three teenagers, were all playing on their cell phones. Not once did they look up and converse with each other. Their phones simply hypnotized them until the food came. Even then, they continued to give their phones full attention while they ate. I thought how sad it was that a family on Christmas Eve could not think of one thing to discuss with each other. I began to wonder what kind of family these children would have one day, being raised by parents who completely ignored them and expected no conversation from them. Sadly, many families follow this same pattern. Too many are connected digitally to the world, but completely disconnected to those who should be the most important people in their world.

Suggestions:

- Do not be the annoying person who talks out loud on your cell phone while in public places, like busses, airports, movie theatres, grocery stores, school campuses, and other similar locations. Most people do not care about your phone conversations.

- Put your phone away during meetings, while on dates, and when you are with friends or family. Certainly, cell phones should be put away while eating with friends or family.

- Parents, remember that your children watch you closely. When you are always on your phone and ignoring them, they will suffer from that behavior. Sadly, they will most likely continue that pattern as adults—doing the same thing with their own children.

- Make sure your phone is on "silent" when you are with others or in public places.

- Do not take incoming calls when you are in face-to-face conversations with others—especially your spouse or children—unless there is an emergency! Likewise, you do not need to respond to text messages when you are in the company of others—unless it is urgent.

- On the other hand, when you receive a text, email, or phone message, respond back to the person who reached out to you in a timely manner. Not responding to others attempts to reach you sends a message anyway. Except this time the message says, "I am ignoring you," or, "I don't care about you."

- Set limits with your children—especially teenagers—of how often they will be on their phones. Have a window of time in the evening with your families where you have "phone free" time, or even a "phone free" zone. For example, between 7:00 p.m. to 9:00 p.m. could be ideal.

- I recommend that you do not let your children sleep in the same room with their cell phones. If they tell you that their phone is their "alarm clock," then you can get them a very inexpensive alarm clock. I recently saw some alarm clocks on *Amazon* for less than $12.

- Monitor your children's phones. Check their phones periodically, ensuring that they are safe and avoiding inappropriate behaviors. Remember parents, you most likely own their phones. Children do not own most cell phones. So do not be afraid to monitor your phone that you are letting them use or take it away when rules are violated.

More on cell phone etiquette

CIVILITY

"Civility carries with it the essence of courtesy, politeness, and consideration for others. All of the education and accomplishments in the world will not count for much unless they are accompanied by marks of gentility, of respect for others, of going the extra mile."
~ Gordon B. Hinckley[16]

Years ago, our family attended a Fourth of July parade in our town. Our community parade is a big deal, and people often camp out on the streets the night before just to have a good view of the parade, which does not begin until the next morning. On this particular occasion, we arrived at 6:30 a.m. to secure our spot, knowing the parade would come right in front of us at about 9:30 a.m. We had set up chairs and blankets in an awesome spot with a perfect view. We had a wonderful morning together, eating, talking, and just relaxing. Before we knew it, we could see the parade coming about 500 yards down the street.

Just then, a family pulled up close to where we were sitting. It seemed about 12 people got out of their large Chevy Suburban and walked over, directly in front of us. With haste, they began to set up their pop-up tent right in front of our family. Essentially, they blocked our entire view of the parade. Just as I was about to say something, my father-in-law spoke up and said, "I'm sorry, but you're going to have to move your tent. Our family has been here for three hours—you can't show up two minutes before the parade and put your tent in front of 20 people." The family was upset, and they left in a huff. However, I believe my father-in-law was right. Some people, I have learned, are not aware of those around them. Such obliviousness is the essence of incivility.

Suggestions:

- Teach your children to be civil by being a civil person. As parents, treat people with courtesy and respect.

- Use respectful language always—your children will notice how you talk to others.

- Be respectful to authority figures such as law enforcement personnel, religious leaders, and the elderly. Teach your children to do the same.

- Teach your children to treat everyone with kindness and respect, regardless of gender, race, religion, height, weight, appearance, or other differences.

- Teach your children to reach out to and protect those who are bullied or marginalized.

- Teach your children what true empathy really is—to walk in another person's shoes for a while.

- Teach your children to control their temper. Teach them

they should not take out their frustrations on others.

- Teach your children to apologize when they are wrong or when they have offended someone.

- Teach your children how to respect others.

- Teach your children to be aware of their surroundings. Do not cut in lines; do not stand in front of people who are trying to see something; do not talk out loud in a movie theatre so those around cannot hear the movie. Essentially, do not behave in a way that demonstrates you are clueless that there are other people in this world besides you.

 *A story about civility*

COLLEGE LIFE

"Economists report that a college education adds many thousands of dollars to a man's lifetime income—which he then spends sending his [children] to college."
~ Bill Vaughan[17]

It is my belief that we should make every sacrifice necessary to obtain a college education. To complete my master's degree, I had to travel from Mesa, Arizona to Flagstaff, Arizona twice a week one fall semester. It was grueling to work all day in Mesa, then drive three hours to Flagstaff, sit in classes for three hours, and then drive home. One summer, in order to finish my degree, I had to live in Flagstaff Monday through Friday, and then I would drive home to Mesa for the weekends to be with Janie and our children. I learned that I could save a lot of money on housing by living in a tent in someone's backyard for the eight-week summer semester. Yes, that is right; I lived in a tent to complete graduate school. How can you beat living anywhere for $25 per month? I recommend that a college education is worth whatever sacrifices need to be made.

Suggestions:

- Do not try to take too many college credits your first year. I see many students who are eager to graduate early before they even take their first class. Their freshman year, they take 16-18 credits and then wonder why their grades are average at best. Go easy on yourself. I recommend that you take 12-14 credits your first semester, and then maybe 14-15 your next semester.

- Enjoy your social life. I believe your social life and the relationships you develop in college are *almost* as important as your education. I am in my late 50s and can honestly say that most of my best friends are individuals I met 30 years ago in college.

- Do not worry about a major until your sophomore year. So many college students feel that they have to declare a major almost immediately, but your mind will change several times—wait until you have been exposed to different courses to declare a major.

- Try to stay ahead of your course schedule. Stay current on reading assignments, papers, and projects. Do not wait until the last minute to get your work done. College is a great time to develop the skill of self-discipline and to overcome procrastination.

- Get involved in university life. Participate in intramurals, clubs, and university activities. Attend speeches and devotionals, as well as athletic events, concerts, plays, and other university events.

- Resist the temptation to skip your classes. In college, you are monitoring yourself. Be disciplined. You will get out of your college experience what you put into it.

 *My favorite college experiences*

COMMON COURTESY

"This is the final test of a gentleman: His respect for those who can be of no possible service to him."
~ William Lyon Phelps[18]

My mom was not a shy person. She always had the confidence to meet people and introduce herself to them. I remember that in every neighborhood we moved into, within a day or two of unpacking, she hit the streets, knocked on doors, and introduced herself to neighbors. It was because of her that we had block parties and neighborhood "get-to-gethers." She taught me much about not waiting for others to come to you. She also taught us to be proactive, kind, and courteous to others.

On the other hand, I had a grandmother who was quite embarrassing. She complained much and treated people rudely. I remember being with her in restaurants and her complaining to the servers often. She would tell them that the food was too hot, or too cold, or that it did not taste right. She was Goldilocks with a bad attitude. She would demand that they fix her meal or give her a refund. This probably would not have been so bad if it happened once or twice, but it happened everywhere we went. I remember my brother and I were so embarrassed. We would practically duck under the table as she was chewing out a young waiter. I remember making a vow to my young teenage self that I would never treat anyone so poorly, and I think I have kept that promise. Sometimes we can learn just as much from a bad example as we can a good one. In my opinion, courtesy is the lubricant that enables every relationship we have to operate smoothly.

Suggestions:

- There are five things you should never do in front of others: 1) cut your toenails, 2) pick your nose, 3) blow your nose, 4) scratch yourself, or 5) change your baby's diaper.

- Be the first to say "hello" to others.

- When new people move into your neighborhood, be one of the first families to welcome them.

- Look people in the eye when you speak to them.

- Be the first to offer a firm handshake.

- Do not interrupt others—let them finish their sentences.

- Always say "thank you," no matter how old you are.

- Be swift to apologize.

- Call people by name and pronounce their name correctly. People love to hear others call them by name.

- Always be kind and respectful to your waiter or server. Tip them generously.

- Do not litter—in fact, pick up litter—even if it is not yours.

When camping or picnicking, never leave any evidence that you were there.

- Leave every place better than you found it—literally every place. When you stay overnight in someone else's home, make the beds, clean the bathrooms and kitchen, and once again, leave the home you have stayed in better than it was when you arrived.

- Do not ever criticize your spouse or children in the presence of others.

- When in groups, introduce individuals to each other. Always introduce your husband, wife, or significant other to those with whom you are associating.

- Always be on time—do not make other people wait for you.

- To echo Jackson Brown's counsel, "When you are the first one up, be quiet about it."[19] I have a friend who loves to wake up at 4:30 a.m. and then make all the noise they possibly can. They are completely unaware that others will be sleeping for another two hours. I assume they believe that if they are awake, everyone else should be awake.

- Never say anything in a text message or email that you would not say to someone face to face.

- When a friend or acquaintance appears in the local paper, cut out the article or photograph and mail it to them.

*Participating with our family at a
local Fourth of July Parade and
Fun 5K Run*

COMMUNITY INVOLVEMENT

"I alone cannot change the world, but I can cast a stone across the waters to create many ripples."
~ *Mother Teresa*[20]

Several years ago, I was sitting up in the stadium during my son's high school football game. At halftime, I began to look around and noticed many people in the bleachers who had no reason to be there. In some cases, they were retired, or in other cases, they did not have children on the football team, on the drill team, or in the band. I began to strike up conversations with many of these people and learned that most of them enjoyed coming to high school football games because it was a community event, and it was their way of supporting their local high school. Some of the older citizens, I learned, had been coming to Texas High School football games for 30 or 40 years. When I saw their example, I hoped that I would follow it.

Suggestions:

- Develop the habit of occasionally checking out your city or community website. There will most likely be a calendar with meetings, events, and fun activities.

- Try to attend high school sporting events, even if you do not have a child playing.

- Find volunteer opportunities. For example, occasionally visit your local fire station and bring dinner and treats to the firefighters and paramedics who are protecting you.

- Vote for those who run for local offices. Put a sign in your yard to support your local candidate. My advice is to vote first and complain later. However, you cannot complain if you have not voted.

- Participate in local parades, rodeos, fairs, carnivals, and other community activities.

- Patronize your local farmer's market.

- Organize an occasional block party in your neighborhood. Be the instigator of pulling your neighbors together and helping them get to know each other.

- Take your children around your neighborhood occasionally to pick up garbage.

- Create a wonderful home atmosphere where families in the area love looking at your house during the Christmas holidays and knocking on your front door on Halloween night. Put another way, do not be the "scary, nutty neighbor."

- Donate your clothing and other household items to Goodwill, Deseret Industries, or the Salvation Army.

COMPUTERS

*"I think it's fair to say that personal computers
have become the most empowering tool we've ever created.
They're tools of communication, they're tools of creativity,
and they can be shaped by their user."*
~ Bill Gates[21]

I once learned a lesson the hard way, which is usually how I learn everything. While working on my master's degree, I was at home on a Saturday afternoon, typing a research paper. I had spent most of the afternoon typing and had created about 20 pages of content. My little son, who was about two years old at the time, was crawling around and playing under the desk where I was typing. All of the sudden, my computer screen went blank, and I instinctively looked under the desk. There, my son was holding the unplugged power cord in his hand. Frantically, I plugged the computer back into the wall and tried to recover my document. This was years ago, before computers had automatic backup features. When I finally got the computer up and running again, the document was completely gone. Four hours of work and 20 pages of text were gone. Lesson #1 with computers—always back up your work! I am sure almost everyone has a similar story to tell.

Suggestions:

- If you have several children, it may be necessary to have more than one computer in your home. At some point, they will all need the computer at the same time for school-work. It is amazing how cheap computers are now—take advantage of good deals found on *Amazon* and *Newegg*.

- Teach your children about the "good" and the "bad" of computers.

- Regularly back up your computer. Portable hard drives are relatively inexpensive these days. I recommend that you store your portable hard drive somewhere else besides your home.

- Keep your family computer in a high-traffic area of the home and monitor your children's computer use. After years in private practice, I recommend that you do not allow your children to have a laptop or any type of computer in their room.

- Limit the amount of time children can spend on computers, and make sure there are consequences when rules are broken.

- Consider installing a program that monitors the internet and can shut it down at night, like *Disney Circle*.

- Consider installing programs on your computer, such as *Net Nanny*, to monitor your child's computer use and the websites they frequent.

- Invest in a reliable anti-virus program.

- Teach your children to avoid clicking on links or sites that they do not recognize.

- Coach your children on sites such as *Amazon* or *eBay* and teach them not to purchase anything without your permission. We once had an 11-year-old daughter purchase a motorcycle on eBay without us knowing. That was a fun day!

 *More computer horror stories*

COST CUTTING

*"Good health, longevity, happiness, a loving family, self-reli-
ance, fine friends... If you have five, you're a rich man..."*
~ Thomas J. Stanley[22]

I have always been amazed that some of the wealthiest
people I have known have lived so frugally. I knew one millionaire dentist who always drove used cars. I know another
millionaire who always purchased his furniture at yard sales.
In fact, one millionaire friend I know actually makes his own
furniture. Many wealthy people have learned to live their lives
on a shoestring budget. Some live in modest homes and blend
in pretty well with the rest of us.

Suggestions:

- Before you can save money, you must know where your
  money is going. Do you know how much money your
  family spends each week/month/year on food, clothing,
  car payments, mortgage, etc.? Purchase a computer program like *Quicken* or *QuickBooks* to track your income
  and expenses.

- Make a household budget, review it often, and stick to it!

- Reduce your grocery bill by 1) not shopping when you are hungry, 2) having a grocery list, and 3) using coupons.

- Meal planning: Eat meals at home, and reserve eating out for special occasions (or once a week). Some meals at restaurants cost more than a weeks' worth of groceries.

- Consider purchasing household items in bulk.

- If you have options, choose an energy provider in your community that will give you the best bang for your buck.

- Banks often charge $15 to $20 per month in fees. Find a bank without maintenance fees. This may mean using a credit union. You can also save money in postage by paying your bills online.

- Pay your bills in a timely manner.

- Avoid paying annual fees on a credit card. To stay out of debt, I recommend that you pay off your credit card balance each month. If you do have high credit card debt, transfer your balance to another card with a zero or low interest rate. You may benefit from consolidating credit card debt.

- If using credit cards, make sure you are taking advantage of "rewards" cards by accumulating "points" for future travel and purchases.

- If you can bundle your internet service with other services, such as cable or satellite TV, then do it! You can often save a significant amount of money.

- If your medical insurance provides a flexible spending account, take advantage. You can save hundreds of dollars per year in taxes.

- Always save for retirement using 401Ks, IRAs, or other pre-tax or tax-sheltered vehicles. This will save you thousands of dollars per year in taxes and allow your savings to grow faster! Take advantage of your employer's "matching funds" program.

- Refinance your home loan to lower the interest rate if you plan to be in the home for a while! I recommend a 15-year fixed mortgage rate; it is amazing how much faster you can pay down your mortgage, and often, the monthly payment is not much more than a 30-year loan.

- Purchase homes that you can fix up and make a profit.

- Teach your children these principles.

CREATING A HEALTHY HOME ENVIRONMENT

"Provide a safe, caring environment for your children. Let them explore. Help them discover. Help them discover the messages and missions inside themselves. They will become something wonderful!
~ Dr. H. Wallace Goddard[23]

My wife, Janie, grew up in a fantastic home environment. Her home was fun and exciting, and many of her peers frequented her home often. Her dad was always making ice cream Sundays and milkshakes in a blender. Her mom was usually making food for everyone. There was always an abundance of laughter and fun. Janie once told me that while in high school, when she was out on dates, she could not wait to get back home. She had FOMO to the max. She knew that her family was having fun, and she was upset that she was missing all the action. What an incredible compliment to parents—that their teenage daughter would rather be with them then on a date with some guy. That is an indicator that parents are doing something right. Many times in Janie's home, all of the children would sit with their parents on their bed. About six cartons of *Blue Bell* ice cream would be open, and each family member had their own spoon. For hours, the family would laugh, talk, and eat ice cream.

Suggestions:

- Purchase a hammock or two and hang them in your back yard. Even use them occasionally! A porch swing can also become a great way to relax and talk to family members.

- Grow a garden and have your children take part in maintaining it. Always work next to your children so that you can visit with and influence each other. Some of the greatest family conversations take place in the yard.

- Listen to music and dance as you work with your family. Listen to good music in your home as often as you can. Share with your children your favorite music and artists.

- Avoid the temptation to have the television on most of the day. I recommend that you only watch programs that you can watch with your whole family. Find ways to limit television viewing and media time.

- Make a tradition of cooking food on a grill regularly.

- Consider having your children share bedrooms. With shared rooms, children learn to cooperate, work together, and talk all night long. What could be better? I would prefer to have my children tired from talking all night long to each other than from playing video games incessantly.

- Create spaces in your home where you and your children can read and have alone time.

- Make the kitchen one of the most favorite places in the home for your family to hang out.

- Adapt to the home environments of others when you visit them. Do not force your home environment on someone else's home. For example, if you are messy, do not assume that the family you are visiting is messy too. Do not inflict your messiness on a family that tries to keep their home tidy.

 *More on home environments*

CRITICISM

"Take care. It is so easy to break eggs without making omelets."
~ C.S. Lewis[24]

Years ago, I was playing in a competitive basketball game. During the course of the game, one of my teammates ran up alongside of me and said in my ear, "Come on man, pick up the pace, you're not helping much." I remember taking issue with my friend and having more of a desire to argue with him than improve my play. His criticism was completely demotivating, and, in my mind, not even valid. After his short little pep talk, I had no desire to improve whatsoever. In fact, I did not even want to continue playing.

However, later in the game, he approached me in the same manner. Except this time, he tried a different approach. He said to me, "Way to hustle. You are shutting the other team down with your defensive play. Keep it up, and we'll follow you." Now that was motivating. Even though I felt I was giving maximum effort, after my teammate's speech, I dug in deeper and gave even more. His message was inspiring, motivating, and gave me a desire to improve. Criticism is one of the most ineffective ways to inspire and lead others. On the other hand, praise and compliments can help the average compete and perform at the highest levels.

Suggestions:

- Do not ever accept criticism from someone whom you would never seek advice from under normal circumstances. This is a great rule for all leaders to follow.

- Remember, criticism rarely inspires people to change their behavior—it just causes them to become mad and resentful.

- I do not believe in the concept of "constructive criticism." I believe that most criticism is destructive.

- Criticism ruins relationships with others. Criticism also destroys trust and respect.

- I second Jackson Brown's advice: "Don't waste time responding to your critics."[25] There are too many people who love us, love what we are doing, and are responsive to us. We should focus on helping, loving, and serving with people who want our help.

- Avoid being critical of others unless they seek for your advice.

- When it comes to criticism, consider the source from which it comes.

- Try to refrain from criticizing anyone for at least a day, if not an entire week. Note how much better you feel!

- Instead of criticizing someone, give them practical ideas that will help them.

• Memorize this little poem: "A good thing to remember and a better thing to do, is work for the construction gang, and not the wrecking crew."

 *More on criticism vs. praise*

DATING IDEAS FOR MARRIED COUPLES

"Babysitters are cheaper than divorces."
~ *Dr. Douglas E. Brinley*[26]

For many years, Janie and I have always had a weekly date night. We found that dating each other was not just a good idea but crucial for growing our marriage. It was a time to get away from the busyness of our lives, to take a break from our children, from emails and texts, and to reconnect with each other. Those dates were an opportunity to remind ourselves of why we were in love in the first place and why we wanted to be with each other for the rest of our lives—and even after that! Often, those dates consisted of going to eat somewhere, going to see a movie, or engaging in some activity. Sometimes we would go out with other couples, which allowed us to connect with others our age. Dating is critical for couples who want to keep their marriages alive and growing.

Suggestions:

- Take turns eating out at each other's favorite restaurant.
- Make dinner for each other and have someone take your kids.

- Go on a picnic.

- Watch a movie in your backyard.

- Go for a bike ride.

- Make a music video.

- Go to a concert or play.

- Take an educational class together.

- Take a dance class together.

- Rent scooters and travel around town.

- Go ice-skating.

- Attend a sporting event together.

- Attend a religious meeting or conference together.

- Play a board game together.

- Play a video game together.

- Go camping.

- Go fishing.

- Do a home project together.

- Read a book together.

- Get a massage together.

- Sit in a hot tub.

- Build something together. This could be food, or a craft, or something your home needs.

- Go through photo albums and share stories with each other.

- Go volunteer to serve together. This could be at an old

folks home or a soup kitchen, or you could go clean up your neighborhood together.

- Video stream a live concert.
- Watch a movie from your high school days together.
- Order food from your favorite restaurant to eat at home.
- Go hiking.
- Go fishing at a fish hatchery.
- Watch your wedding video.
- Dance to music from the days when you first met.
- Rent a tandem bike and ride it together.
- Ride motorcycles together.
- Go to a health club or fitness center and work out together.
- Go visit some hot springs.
- Make Dutch oven peach cobbler in your back yard.
- Go bowling.
- Go shopping.
- Go on a walk.
- Get ice cream cones.
- Ride go-carts.
- Fly kites together.
- Feed the ducks at a park.
- Play on a playground together—but do not act creepy.
- Float down a river on inner tubes.

- Do random acts of kindness for other people.
- Make cookies and deliver them to people in your neighborhood.
- Wash your cars together.
- Rent some wave runners.
- Miniature golf together.
- Go horseback riding.
- Attend a professional sporting event together.
- Go to a furniture store and pretend you can buy anything you want.
- Make a campfire and roast marshmallows.
- Make ice cream Sundays.
- Have a picnic in the back of your pickup truck.
- Go look at incredible dream homes together.
- Design your dream cabin together.
- Put a puzzle together.
- Go to the best milkshake place in town.
- Play pickle ball.
- Play ping-pong
- Throw a Frisbee.
- Play croquet.
- Play badminton.
- Go skeet shooting.

DISCIPLINE

"However—and this is a painful psychological truth—our primary responsibility is not to gratify our children (which of course we do often, and happily), but to make certain that they develop a repertoire of skills that will help them meet life's inevitable challenges and disappointments."
~ Dr. Madeline Levine[27]

For me, it is hard to think about the concept of discipline without thinking of my daughter Brittany. From the time she was young, she seemed to regulate herself well. She woke up to her own alarm clock at an early age. As our oldest daughter, she would help Janie dress the other children, change their diapers, and even vacuum floors. As a teenager, she would wake up early for a religious class taught at our church, and then she would go to cross country practice. She would come home from high school and then go to work at an orthodontics office for several hours. She would do her homework in the evening and then begin the same routine again the next day. She practically paid for her entire college education on her own. As the mother of five children, she continues to work out daily and run marathons. One day, I hope to become more like her.

If parents want disciplined children, they must model self-discipline. For example, if a parent spends their life watching television or playing video games while eating junk food and spilling the crumbs all over their bodies, their children will have a difficult time becoming disciplined individuals. If your home is constantly a wreck and there are dishes in your sink from last month, there is a good chance your children will not learn the skill of discipline.

Suggestions:

- Teach your children what it means to be disciplined. Essentially, it means to be in control of your life. Being disciplined suggests that you do not succumb to the tendencies of laziness, apathy, rudeness, tardiness, procrastination, lack of impulse control, irritability, anger, foul language, disorganization, negativity, and immediate gratification. Those who are disciplined grab life by the horns and take charge. I love this definition: "The disciplined person picks up his clothes; the undisciplined lets them lie. One washes the bathtub after himself; the other leaves the high-water mark for someone else to scrub. One plans his work and works his plan; the other works haphazardly. One is habitually prompt in his appointments; the other is notoriously tardy. Some people are always on time to church, while others never are. Observers of many years' experience will support the claim that the difference cannot be explained in the greater distance to travel or the larger families to hustle. The difference is habit, and habit is character."[28]

- Many adolescents today have lost the skill of self-discipline. Unfortunately, they lack role models in this area. Some adults lack the discipline to detach themselves from their cell phones to connect with their children. Parents *can be* great models of self-discipline for their children simply by disconnecting themselves from their own addictions.

- Teach your children that without discipline, goals will not be attained, and potential will be squandered. Without discipline, jobs and careers will be inconsistent and unfulfilling; without discipline, their own health could become jeopardized; without discipline, their future marriage and family life will be difficult and frustrating; without discipline, their spiritual life will be non-existent; without discipline, bad habits and addictions will take root and blossom. Without discipline, neither they nor their children will be able to be successful in life!

- Teach your children that discipline begins with the simple things; teach them to clean their clothes off the floor, make their bed, brush their teeth, put their shoes where they belong, and to put their toys back where they found them. At an early age, teach them to dress themselves, tie their own shoes, and make their beds.

- Teach your children to be punctual. Being late to events essentially says, "I don't really care about this." Live by the mantra, "If you are not five minutes early, then you are late."

- Teach them to accomplish their duties without being told, like their chores, homework, and piano practice. Have them establish routines and become self-starters.

- Teach your children to save their money. Have them identify something big they would like to save their money for and purchase. Encourage them to not let their money "burn a hole in their pocket."

- Parents, clean up after yourselves. If you have some garbage, throw it in the wastebasket. If you have clothes on the floor, pick them up. Do not leave your dishes on the table or in your bedroom! Take them to the sink and wash them. Discipline means caring more about others than yourself.

- Unpack your suitcase as soon as you arrive home from a trip—do not wait for three days to get around to that.

- Make sure your room is clean and your bed is made each day.

Our daughter, Brittany, began running in middle school. As the mother of five, she continues to run competitively today. I have enjoyed viewing from a distance the process Brittany engages in to train for such races. Pure discipline, that is for sure.

 *More on discipline*

DRIVING

"Leave sooner,
Drive slower,
Live longer."
~ Anonymous[29]

For me, there is nothing much better than a drive across the country. I prefer some good country music to sing aloud. I like the windows rolled down so that I can chew on sunflower seeds and spit them out the window. Of course, I need a good drink to keep me alert and focused. Additionally, if my family wants to come, well, that is an added bonus. Driving the back roads of America has always been a therapeutic exercise for me. Driving with my children for long distances has been an entirely different exercise—sometimes an exercise of patience.

One of my favorite childhood memories was going for Sunday drives with my family. One of my favorite memories in my adult life has been the many trips that our family has taken—mostly driving from one part of the country to the other. Some of the greatest family memories can take place in our cars.

Suggestions:

- Be a courteous driver and obey traffic laws. When other drivers need to get into the lane you are in, let them in.

- When driving on a freeway or interstate, only use the left lane for passing. Do not get in the left lane and then drive 45 miles per hour. *Drive on the right, pass on the left!* This is one of the most misunderstood driving concepts in the United States of America.

- Avoid the temptation to text while driving. If you need to respond to a text, pull over. Most of our children have wrecked one of our cars by texting while they drove.

- Do not drive when you are tired/exhausted! Do not drive fast in rain or snowy conditions—slow down!

- Have an emergency kit in the trunk of your car, complete with flashlights, jumper cables, blankets, and other helpful equipment.

- Consider the following maintenance on your car: wash your cars at least monthly; take the garbage out of your car at the end of each day; have the oil changed on your car every three months, or 3,000 miles.

- Teach your children that driving is a privilege, not a right. Our teenagers needed to demonstrate maturity and responsibility before they were allowed to drive.

EDUCATION

"The education of a man is never completed until he dies."
~ Robert E. Lee[30]

I did not do that well in high school. For me, school was primarily a social experience, and I did not study that hard. However, my high school counselor made a huge mistake. She told me that my grades were probably too poor to attend college. Instead of pursuing a college education, she recommended that I should consider a career in the military or learn a trade. Since I am a competitive person, I decided I would show her. I graduated from college with some honors in my undergraduate program of organizational behavior. Afterwards, I received a master's degree in educational psychology, and then a second master's degree in mental health counseling. Finally, I earned a Ph.D. in family and human development.

My point: Do not judge your children by how they perform in middle school and even high school. If their desire is strong, encourage them to pursue their dreams. I never dreamed as a high school student that I would one day become a university professor. My dream unfolded one layer at a time as I continued to pursue my education. Ironically, I made better grades in my doctoral program than I did in middle school. Never give up on your children. I wish I could reconnect with my high school counselor and let her know what she motivated me to accomplish. I would thank her for inspiring me to make more of myself than I thought (and she thought) was possible. Education is the key that can unlock our dreams.

Suggestions:

- Have the attitude that you can learn something from everyone you meet. Regardless of if they are a neurosurgeon or blue-collar employee.

- Have a desire to continue learning new things throughout your life. When you are through learning, you are through living. Never let your mind go stagnant. Read, watch educational videos, and pick the brains of those who know more than you do.

- When you meet people from other cultures, learn as much about their native country and customs as you can. Ask these individuals questions about their native land—they will appreciate you for taking time to learn more about them and their homeland. Learn to give greetings in several different languages.

- Some of the most successful people read books regularly. If you want to gain an advantage in life, both personally and professionally, then read! Find ways to read while you walk on a treadmill or ride an exercise bike. Read something uplifting each night before you go to bed and each morning after waking up.

- Memorize several killer poems.

- Consider attending graduate school to obtain a masters or doctorate degree. The higher degree you have, the more doors will open for you. Moreover, the higher degree you have, the more money you will make.

- Ask questions of those who know more than you. Try to come to understand what they have learned from their own experiences.

- Watch YouTube videos on how to fix things around your home and on how to build things. Create your own "do-it-yourself" video for the public. Share your knowledge with others.

- Listen to podcasts on topics that interest you. Consider creating your own podcast to share the information you have gleaned.

- Take an interest in your children's education. Be involved in their homework, attend parent-teacher conferences, review their report cards together, and set educational goals with them.

Graduation with my Ph.D. from Utah State University, May 2000, at the ripe old age of 37. Janie and I had been married for 15 years and had seven children by the time I had finished school. We do not recommend that program!

ESSENTIALS FOR A HOME

"One's home is the safest refuge to everyone."
~ Pandects[31]

When I was in elementary school in the early 1970s, I remember my mom taking my siblings and me to her friend's home in the Texas Hill country. I recall going into their large backyard with every imaginable contraption for kids. There was a pool, a trampoline, a treehouse, a springboard, and a rope swing that could take you across a dry creek bed. I had never seen a backyard like this, but I decided on that occasion that when I became a parent, I would have such a backyard for my own children. Janie and I always wanted to create an environment where our children wanted to be home—not at the neighbor's house down the street, the skating rink, or the bowling alley. Many years later, we lived in Mesa, Arizona. In that backyard, there was a pool, a trampoline, and a large swing set. We even had a porch swing hanging from a tree. As a young father, I loved looking into my backyard and watching my children play with each other. Often, other children from the neighborhood came to our home, and that was okay too. I even remember the time we placed our trampoline next to the pool so that we could jump extra high before hitting the water. Even to this day, that was my favorite home. Although it was our smallest home, there was so much for our children to do!

Suggestions:

Consider having the following in your home:

- A library full of wonderful books, along with a quiet place for family members to think, write, ponder, or do homework.

- A nice, large kitchen table that can accommodate many people and serve as a gathering place.

- A nice blender/juicer, an ice cream maker, and a waffle iron.

- A fireplace.

- A basketball hoop.

- A trampoline.

- A ping-pong table.

- A large yard with plenty of room to run around and play.

- A picnic table in the backyard or on a deck.

- A backyard hammock.

- Plenty of storage space.

- A big-screen, high-definition television.

- Enough computers for children to complete their homework.

- A grill or smoker.

ESSENTIALS FOR YOUR FAMILY

*"Every house where love abides and friendship
is a guest, is surely home, and home, sweet home;
For there the heart can rest."*
~ Henry van Dyke[32]

Until recently, everywhere we have lived—Arizona, Utah, and Texas, I have had to make friends with a neighbor who had a pickup truck. It seemed that many weekends; we needed a pick-up truck for something. We seemed to be that family that was always taking something to the dump, hauling tree limbs out of our yard, or going to pick up some topsoil to spread on our lawn. I always disliked having to borrow a truck from someone else. One of the greatest days of my life is when I purchased my own pickup truck. Now the tables have turned. It seems that everyone wants to borrow my truck. Therefore, I am contemplating purchasing an old, used, banged-up pickup for the neighbors to borrow. Such is the circle of life.

Suggestions:

Consider the goal for your home or future home to include some of the following (if possible):

- A pick-up truck—even if it is old and used, you will need it often.

- A good, complete first aid kit.

- A garden.

- Camping equipment. This means tents, air mattresses, portable stoves, containers for water storage, flashlights, and sleeping bags.

- Indoor games such as board games or other games the family can play. Consider also outdoor games such as croquet, badminton, or even volleyball.

- A pet.

- A utility trailer for hauling things or for moving things around.

- A scale.

- Yard equipment, such as mowers, weed eaters, hedge clippers, wheelbarrows, and a pruning saw.

- Hand tools and power tools, a chain saw, and a sturdy, tall ladder.

EXERCISE

"To preserve health is a moral and religious duty, for health
is the basis of all social virtues.
We can no longer be useful when not well."
~ Samuel Johnson[33]

I am not sure if there is a better way to begin the day than with some exercise. To wake up early and hit the gym, the bike, the trail, or even the pavement is a first-rate accomplishment each day. As I jog in the morning, or even walk, it is a time to think, to process, to problem solve, and even to count my many blessings.

When Janie and I first started dating, we jogged often and played racquetball at least weekly. I remembered thinking how great life would be once we were married. In my fantasy world, our married life would consist of waking up together at 6:00 a.m., reading our scriptures together, jogging with each other down the tree-lined streets of our college town, eating a wonderful breakfast together, and leaving for work or school by 8:00 a.m. I had every reason to believe that after about ten years of marriage, we would instill this same pattern into the lives of all of our able-bodied children. Not only would Janie and I jog together, but our eight children would be jogging behind us, in single file. I imagined that we would all be wearing matching jogging suits and whistling as we made our way down the lane of our beautiful neighborhood.

However, that is not what happened. Shortly after our honeymoon, we returned to Provo in April to begin our summer jobs as we tried to save money for fall tuition. The day after we moved into our student basement apartment just south of the Brigham Young University Campus, I suggested to Janie that we wake up early and go jogging. Dutifully, Janie accompanied me on our morning run, but I could tell that she was not really "into it." After about a mile, we stopped and she confessed her major transgression. She said, "There is something I need to tell you." I braced myself for the worst and said, "Go ahead." Janie admitted, "I actually hate jogging. I simply do not like it at all. Never have, and never will." I was confused because we had jogged so often during our engagement. Therefore, I asked the obvious question, "Janie, why have you jogged with me almost daily the past six months?" She said, "Because I wanted to be with you, and I knew that you liked it when I jogged with you. Now that we are married, I need to come clean. I abhor jogging, and worse than that, I do not like waking up at 6:00 a.m. either." Wow, I was stunned. My whole plan of having a jogging family with matching sweat pants was just flushed down the toilet. However, I loved Janie very much, and I knew that this would not be a deal breaker. After all, it was not that she was throwing *all* exercise out the window. She explained to me that she still wanted to do aerobics and dance classes, but she simply did not like to run. I had to lower my expectations in this area and realize that my new bride was different from me. The more I thought about it, the more I knew I needed to relax my expectation and find other activities that we could do together.

Suggestions:

- Make sure you are involved in cardiovascular exercise until you simply cannot do it anymore. There are so many mental health and emotional health benefits to 30 minutes of cardio exercise daily. This type of exercise reduces stress, releases endorphins, strengthens your heart, and helps you manage stress better.

- Exercise will help you feel much better about yourself and your sense of accomplishment. It can be an esteem booster. When exercising, we feel much better!

- If possible, purchase a membership at a health club for your family. There are too many health options for your family to pass up, and it is something you can enjoy doing together.

- Take up a sport that you can play with your family, like racquetball, badminton, tennis, or golf. Play sports and games in your backyard, like racquetball, badminton, pickle ball, tennis, or golf.

- Consider multitasking when you exercise. You can read while on a recumbent bike. You can listen to a podcast while you jog. You can listen to something educational while you lift weights. I have discovered that I can read

10-15 books a year because I can read while I exercise.

- Engage in stretching or yoga as often as you can, especially when you get older.

FAMILY VACATIONS

"The greatest legacy we can leave
our children is happy memories."
~ Og Mandino[34]

Perhaps we as Americans use the term "vacation" too loosely. My wife has often said that if the children come along—it is no longer a vacation. There is often no downtime for parents on a family vacation. In fact, parents may feel more stress on a vacation then when the family is at home. My wife is insistent that when the children come along, it should be called "a family trip."

On another occasion, our family was moving from Logan, Utah to Dallas, Texas. An acquaintance at the university where I was a student heard that we were moving and wanted to help. They understood it was a long drive from Utah to Texas, and they knew we had seven children. In an attempt to help, this person handed me a toy glass eye. I asked what that was, and they said, "I know you have a long way to drive, and I thought if your children got a little rowdy in the car, they could play with this toy." I tried not to laugh. Even in 1999, we had videos to watch in our cars and other means to keep our children entertained. I do not think that toy glass eye would have helped. In fact, I am not even sure a glass eye would have kept me entertained when I was a kid back in the 70s. I am sure my brother and I would have found a way to toss it out the window at another car. I appreciated this person's desire to help us, but their suggestion was so off base, it was humorous.

Suggestions:

- Consider paying for family vacations in cash—you will enjoy your time together if you do not have to spend the rest of the year paying off your "little trip." However, if paying in cash, enjoy yourselves! If you are constantly worried about the cost, you may miss the rich blessings of being with your children. It is more important to make memories on such trips that will last a lifetime!

- Plan several family vacations or trips each year. These do not always need to be expensive. Every family needs to get away from the rat race, unplug from the grid, and make family memories together. This could mean something as simple as a two-day camping trip.

- When going on trips, avoid the temptation to "drive straight through." We did that for years, and it can be punishing. Spend the extra money and get a hotel. You can sleep and shower.

- Consider not being in a hurry while on trips. Perhaps enjoy taking your time getting to your destination, taking side journeys, and enjoying scenery and the fun things to do along the way. Sometimes we get so focused on "just getting there" that we miss the amazing experiences and opportunities along the way. My wife, Janie, feels that we should have taken this approach more often, but I was always so concerned about getting back to work. Okay, I am the biggest hypocrite for recommending this, but you all could turn out better than me!

- Document your trips and vacations with journals and photographs.

- Recognize that on trips, you often need to eat dinner early and go to bed early. Often, we press too hard and try to shove too much fun into small windows of time. Take your time, slow down, and relax—you are on vacation! Recognize your limits and your children's limits.

- Have your children help you with the planning of family trips.

- If traveling long distances in the car, find ways to make car travel fun. Movies can certainly help, but there are games and other activities that can make the trip fun.

- Learn to be flexible and teach your kids to be flexible.

- Find ways to spend one-on-one time with your spouse and with each of your children while on trips and vacations.

- Make sure that your family understands the purpose of the trip: to be together, to enjoy each other's company, and to bond closer together. Often, on such trips, some family members want to remain distant from the family or do their own thing.

- Create fun traditions on your trips and vacations.
- Make sure everyone helps and works together as a team.[35]

Some interesting vacation experiences

FEAR

"If you acted on all the fears concerning your children, you'd have to spend so much energy trying to protect them that you wouldn't have time to raise them."
~ *Liat Collins*[36]

I have been a worrier most of my life. My mom was a worrier, and her father, my granddad, was a worrier. The worry gene is in my blood, and unfortunately, I have passed it down to some of my children. Here is the lesson I would like to pass down to the next generation. Most of the things I have devoted mental energy to in worrying have never happened. In fact, I believe that about 95 percent of the things I have worried about have never transpired. Worrying is such a waste of time! My theory: we can live our lives from two paradigms: we can live our lives out of fear, or we can live out of love. A life lived with a backdrop of love is much happier and fulfilling than a life lived out of fear. Take my word for it.

Suggestions:

- Fear is *False Evidence Appearing Real*. Most of the things we fear are not based on strong evidence—they are based most often on false assumptions.

- Most of the things we worry about never happen. I recommend that you do not take counsel from your fears.

- Do not make decisions based on fear.

- In Jackson Brown's words, "Remember that almost everything looks better after a good night's sleep."[37]

- Do not engage in "What if?" thinking. If you spend all of your time in fear, you will have no time to live in happiness.

- Do not waste a good worry. Do not worry about things you have no control over.

- Challenge every negative and fearful thought you have. Replace every negative, fearful thought with something more positive. Indeed, fill your mind with faith, hope, and optimism.

- Do not believe everything you hear, and certainly do not believe everything you read on social media or the internet. Give your children hope; bless them with the gift of faith.

- Those who fear often become control freaks. Trust in God and yield your control to Him.

- One great remedy for worry: serve and help other people—get your mind off your own troubles!

- Another remedy for worry is this: be grateful. Focus on what you do have, instead of what you lack. As Dennis Prager points out, "All happy people are grateful, and ungrateful people cannot be happy."[38]

- To stay on track, try the following experiment. Keep a journal daily, and each evening, address the following questions with a brief response:

    1. Was there something funny that happened to you today?

    2. What were you successful at today?

    3. What are you grateful for today?

    4. How did God touch your life today?

 *More on fear*

FINANCES

"Debt is so ingrained into our culture that most Americans can't even envision a car without a payment, a house without a mortgage, a student without a loan, a credit without a card."
~ Dave Ramsey[39]

I am a big fan of budgets. I look back on our life and sometimes wonder how we survived financially. We had a large family and a modest income. However, I believe what made things work for us monetarily was living off a strict budget. Budgets force us to be disciplined and accountable—something every household needs to be financially successful.

Suggestions:

- Read Dave Ramsey's *The Total Money Makeover* together as a couple. Then, make a financial plan for your life. Another great book for a financial education: *The Millionaire Next Door* by Thomas J. Stanley and William D. Danko.

- Pay the Lord first—pay your tithes and offerings before you pay anything else.

- Pay yourself second—put 10-20 percent of your income into some form of savings.

- Work towards saving $1,000 for an emergency fund, and then expand that to a three- to six-month emergency fund that you could live on.

- Live on a strict budget. Some individuals live by a 50/30/20 rule, where you live off 50 percent of your income; 30 percent goes to wants, vacations, entertainment, and things like that, and 20 percent is devoted to savings and investments. Track every dollar you spend!

- Keep your receipts. Especially food and gas receipts if you travel with work.

- Begin saving for your children's education as soon as you can.

- Have a healthy life insurance policy. Experts suggest that it should be six times your household income. It is somewhat surprising how cheap such policies can be.

- Have a strong health insurance plan. Make sure you have adequate coverage for your entire family.

- Stay out of debt—try to avoid it like the plague. I would recommend that you do not use credit cards unless you absolutely must! In our modern world, you can purchase plane tickets, hotels, and just about anything else with a debit card.

- When in debt, use the snowball approach to pay your debts off quickly, starting with the smallest debt, and working up to the largest (see www.ramseysolutions.com/debt/how-the-debt-snowball-method-works).

- If you decide to use a credit card, only do it as a matter of convenience and to accumulate points but never because you do not have the money to make a purchase.

- Work towards home ownership. A 15-year mortgage can do miracles for your financial future. Have a fixed mortgage rate. Adjustable rates can lead to financial disaster if you are not careful. Take my word for it! Been there, done that, and bought the T-shirt!

- If your employer has a matching funds program, take full advantage of that! Max the match on your 401K. If your employer will pay up to 6 percent, then work your way to matching that.

- Consider having separate checking accounts for you and your spouse. As a couple, you may manage finances very differently, and this practice helps. Many people suggest that married couples should have a joint account, but I view this very differently. Each spouse in the marriage should be mature enough to manage his or her own account. Because our personalities are different, the way we manage money is different. Separate checking accounts can help us avoid a multitude of financial challenges.

- Even if you are wealthy, do not allow your children know it—wealth is great for some adults but can ruin most children. No matter how wealthy you are, teach your children how to work, how to save, and how to live frugally. Have your children be responsible for paying for some of their needs, clothes, camps, phones, and even car insurance.

- One wise man counseled, "Never invest more in the stock market than you can afford to lose."[40]

- Never believe the "check is in the mail." Never believe a deal is done or that you have made money on a transaction until the check has cleared in your bank account!

- Never make large purchases in haste. Always take time to think and consider the positive and negative ramifications of your choice. "Sleeping on it," is always a good practice. Praying over it is even better.

- Be leery about lending money to friends, borrowing money from friends, or going into business with a friend or even a family member. On many occasions, these relationships can work, and work well. However, when they do not work, they can ruin relationships for a lifetime.

- Think twice before co-signing on a loan.

- Create a financial vision board.

FRIENDSHIPS

"Have good associates or don't associate at all. Be careful in the selection of your friends. If in the presence of certain persons you are lifted to nobler heights, you are in good company"
~ Ezra Taft Benson[41]

One of the great blessings in my life has been having incredible friends. In high school, I had a set of friends who had high moral standards, and they kept me out of trouble. I learned from them that I could have fun in wholesome ways—something most of my high school associates did not understand. In college, I had wonderful friends—many of them are still close friends today—and now we are grandparents together. We bonded during those college days because most of us were in the same boat—we had little money, less time, and mega stress. We learned that despite those challenges, we could have incredible, fun times together. In other places we have lived, we have met awesome, close friends. Often, these have been other married couples. What we had in common was that we were raising our children together. As we experienced similar challenges, we supported each other and had so much fun together. What would life be like without great friends?

Suggestions:

- Everyone needs awesome friends. Friends can be a great source of strength and support.

- Good friends can be a great mental health outlet. Friends can help us focus on the fun parts of life, they can help us de-stress, and they can help us find happiness and joy.

- Teach your children to keep good company—encourage them to choose friends who share their values, beliefs, and standards.

- Friends can keep us safe, help us resist temptation, and influence us for good. These friends protect us and want to help us. Friends can also push us to try new things and to get out of our comfort zones.

- According to Ralph Waldo Emerson, the only way to have a friend is to be one.

- Keep in touch with your friends over the years—you may discover that you need their help years down the road, or they may need help from you.

- True friends may not see each other for 20 years, but when they do reconnect, they can pick up right where they left off as if they have never been apart.

- Good friends are good listeners, and they understand us.

- Good friends support us in our dreams, goals, and visions of the future.

- Good friends accept us, as we are, warts and all.

- Good friends always have our back.

- Good friends can help us through difficult times, trauma, loss, and even death.

- Good friends can inspire us to do well.

- Good friends see the good in us when others may not.

 *The power of healthy friendships*

FUN

*"The best way to keep children home is
to make the home atmosphere pleasant—and let the
air out of the tires."
~ Dorothy Parker[42]*

Years ago, when we lived in the Dallas area, some good friends of ours from the Western United States came to visit us. As two families, we sat in our large family room and planned a few things we would do while our friends were in town with us. One of the most popular attractions in the Dallas/Ft. Worth area is Six Flags Over Texas—an incredible amusement park. Our oldest daughter suggested that on one of our days together, we visit the famed amusement park. Noticing that our friends did not seem too excited, our oldest daughter began to tell the family about several incredible rollercoasters in the theme park. Still, appearing unimpressed, our daughter said, "So, let me guess, you all are not the 'rollercoaster type.'" Our friends laughed at that idea and assured us that they enjoyed rollercoasters as much as anyone did. A few days later, we found ourselves at Six Flags, and, to this day, I am grateful that our friends certainly were the "rollercoaster type." We all had a great time together in the Texas heat. From that experience and many others, I was grateful that along with my wife, Janie, we did our best to create a fun culture in our home. Our children knew that we were going to have some fun. We wanted our kids to laugh, we wanted them to enjoy themselves, and we wanted them to have fun with each other. We always believed that "a family who plays together stays together." Research shows that wholesome recreation in families helps children to build both virtuous and happy lives. Wholesome recreation also creates memories that can last a lifetime.

Suggestions:

- Play in the rain with your kids.
- Play hide-n-go-seek with your children, indoors or outdoors.
- Never let a good snowstorm go without your family getting a little wet and icy.
- Ride rollercoasters and visit amusement parks often.
- Camp and hike together.
- Take your children swimming and to water parks.
- Sing with your family, aloud and together.
- Fly kites together.
- Play board games or card games together.
- Put puzzles together.
- Go to the lake.

- Go to the beach.

- Have backyard barbeques.

- Make homemade ice cream.

- Watch funny shows and movies together. Have a movie night in your backyard.

- Play croquet, volleyball, and badminton in your backyard.

- Go bowling.

- Go roller-skating.

- Go to amusement parks.

- Eat out together.

- Go on family walks.

- Go on family bike rides.

- Create a family mural in your driveway.

- Play basketball or pickle ball in your driveway.

- Play whiffle ball.

- Play in your sprinkler.

- Play miniature golf.

- Get a hot tub.

- Fun does not always automatically happen. Therefore, make it happen! Deliberately "make fun" a part of your family culture.

Janie and the girls enjoying the California Beach.

GOALS

"Did you know that less than two percent of Americans set goals or have written plans for their lives? However, 95 percent of all successful business executives have written goals. The other 98 percent who do not have written goals for themselves usually work for those who do."
~ Dr. Randal Wright[43]

I remember the first time I really set goals in my life. As an undergraduate student, I wanted to leave a smaller school in Texas to transfer to a more prestigious academic institution in the intermountain west. However, after my first semester in college, my GPA took a nosedive. Therefore, for the first time in my life, I sat down and wrote down some specific goals, which included being admitted to the other University that I desired to attend. I knew that I had to make the best grades of my life that second semester in college if I was going to have any chance of transferring. So, that second semester, I really was "dialed in." I took fewer classes and studied harder than I ever had. I also set some physical and spiritual goals at that time. By end of the semester, every goal that I had set had been accomplished, including being accepted to the college of my dreams. I learned that if we set goals and review them often, miracles can occur in our lives.

Suggestions:

- Share with your children your own experiences of setting goals, working hard, and achieving dreams. Let them know of your failures and hard lessons as well.

- Teach your children that if they want to have a fulfilling life, they must plan their lives. Most of the good things in life are not due to happenstance. They come from dreaming dreams, setting goals, and working towards their fulfillment.

- Teach your children that most people who have written goals accomplish the most in this life.

- Help your children set goals for life. Write them up and consider framing them to make them easy to review often.

- Have monthly interviews with your children to review their goals. Follow up is critical!

- Help your children discover their mission in life. Help them grasp their purpose, their gifts, and their talents.

- Help your children develop a list of 20 things that they love to do. This will help them identify their gifts, talents, and passions.

- Help your children create a vision board with their goals, dreams, and aspirations. Have it hang on their bedroom wall.

- Each day, look for ways to improve your marriage, your relationships with your children, and your bank account. Once you accomplish your goals, set new ones that cause you to stretch and grow.

- Have a "bucket list." Keep this list in a location where you can see it and review it often. One of our daughters keeps this list on her phone. Identify 50 to 100 things you would like to experience before you die.

 *More on goals*

GRATITUDE

"One heartfelt thank-you will suck the oxygen out of worry's world. So, say it often. Focus more on what you do have and less on what you don't."
~ Max Lucado[44]

I believe that one of the most seminal experiences that I have ever had in life was writing a thank you note. I wrote the note to a man many who died about 20 years ago. He was an inspirational speaker of sorts, and back in the early 1980s, I listened to many of his cassette tape recordings as I lay in a hospital bed with a broken pelvis.

His messages inspired me and gave me great hope and confidence that I would heal and make a complete recovery, which I did. Years later, I found the man's address and wrote him a letter—thanking him for what he had done for me. A tender part of this story is that despite his age and feeble condition, he wrote me back, thanking me for making his day. I learned that just a few weeks later, this man passed away. I was grateful I was able to reach out to him and show my gratitude before his death. It is never too late to tell someone thank you.

Suggestions:

- Teach your children to say "please" and "thank you" to others—especially to adults who do things for them like give them rides home from school or practice.

- Do not ever feel that writing an old-fashioned thank you note is out of date. Always thank people for gifts with a note or a card. When you receive wedding gifts, make sure that you write those most important thank you notes— even if it takes a year to complete them!

- At the end of each school year, have your children, and yourself, write a thank you note to a teacher who has made a difference in their life.

- Occasionally, locate one of your old schoolteachers, coaches, church leaders, or professors, and write them a thank you note. Express to them how they made a difference in your life. It will make their day—maybe even their week.

- Write thank you notes and make cookies for police officers, paramedics, and firefighters. Show up to their station and thank them personally.

- When you see a military person, thank them for their service.

- Make it a practice in your family to count your blessings often. Create an "attitude of gratitude" in your family culture. Write your blessings out on a poster board for all to see.

- As you become an adult, find ways to express gratitude to your parents for the so many things they did for you at different points in your life.

- Teach your family that one of the great remedies for stress and anxiety is to focus on gratitude. In fact, gratitude is the secret to happiness.

- Keep an individual or family gratitude journal.

- At the end of each day, consider three things for which you are grateful.

- Quoting Jackson Brown, "Understand that happiness is not based on possessions, power, or prestige, but on relationships with people you love and respect."[45]

 *More on one of Mark's favorite topics: gratitude*

GRIT

"By allowing [our children] to get occasionally bruised in child-hood, we are helping to make certain that they don't get broken in adolescence. And by allowing them their failures in adolescence, we are helping to lay the groundwork for success in adulthood."
~ *Dr. Madeline Levine*[46]

I think that "grit" is one of the most admirable traits in a person. When I think of grit, I automatically think of my son, Brandon. He was an all-state linebacker in Texas. Consequently, he was recruited by several colleges but chose to attend Brigham Young University to play football. When he arrived on campus, the coaches did not take him that seriously. At 5'11" and 225 pounds, he was an undersized middle linebacker. However, during his freshman year, after the spring camp, he had caught the attention of the coaches. Perhaps he could play special teams, maybe even make his way on to the depth chart—albeit third or fourth string. But he had something the coaches did not know about—grit.

As a freshman, he became one of the most significant special teams' players on the roster. By his sophomore season, he started at inside linebacker. He led his team in tackles his junior and senior year. He was ultimately elected team captain. He played through major injuries and never came off the field. He was not as big physically as his teammates, and some even thought he was too slow to play his position. He proved everyone wrong because of his powerful work ethic and because of his grit.

Suggestions:

- Teach your children that life is often hard—but hard is good—hard is what makes us into strong men and women. Help them understand that it takes resistance to build strong men and women of character.

- Teach your children to be "gritty." Grit is a combination of passion, perseverance, and self-discipline that will help them keep moving forward in spite of obstacles.[47]

- Teach your children that if they have grit, they have the potential to outperform those who are brighter, more talented, more skilled, and more gifted. Grit can trump everything.

- Teach your children that grit is born from an incredible work ethic and desire to achieve. Without work ethic and desire, grit does not exist.

- Never do anything for your children that they can do for themselves.

- Allow your children to fail. Stay out of the way of some

of life's most important lessons. And when they do fail, be the first one to help pick them up, love them, and encourage them.

- If parents wish to teach their children to have grit, they must be gritty themselves. Parents cannot wilt under pressure, curl up in the fetal position, or fall on the ground and cry each time something goes wrong in their lives. They must face challenges head on, fearless, ready to take on the world.

- Do your children know your grit stories? I would recommend that you share your "gritty" experiences with your children often.

- Help your children identify grit stories in history, literature, and from their ancestry.

- Consider teaching your children that quitting is not allowed. Occasionally, there will be exceptions to this rule. Under certain circumstances, teach your children that if they want to "discontinue" football, soccer, band, choir, swimming, or the academic decathlon, they can, but they must wait until the season is over. No quitting mid-stream.

- When your children fall off the proverbial horse, help them up, dust them off, and then put them back on that horse again.

- Expect your children to do hard things. Put challenges in front of them. Create opportunities for them to develop grit.

- Praise your children and acknowledge their grit.

- Encourage your children to take risks and to do things outside of their comfort zone.

Brandon was known as one of the "grittiest" linebackers on the Brigham Young University football team. I loved watching him play with such intensity. Even though it has been almost 10 years since his last college bowl game, I still have fans approach me and say, "We sure miss watching Brandon Ogletree play linebacker." I tell them that I do as well.

HAPPINESS

"Too much anxious opening of the oven door and the cake falls instead of rising. So it is with us. If we are always selfishly taking our temperatures to see if we are happy, we will not be."
~ Neal A. Maxwell[48]

Happiness, in my mind, comes from what we choose to focus on in life. If we are always focused on problems, pains, politics, and so many other issues that are out of our control, we will never be happy. Years ago, I knew a man in Mesa, Arizona who attended Church with us. I noticed that he was always happy. This man was constantly smiling, always had a good joke or story to share, and seemed to be in the best mood. I was practically dumbfounded when I learned that his wife was dying of a terminal illness. In fact, one of this man's only respites was when he could attend church once a week and mingle for a brief time with other faith-filled people. This man taught me that happiness does not need to be directly attached to our circumstances. In fact, we can be happy, no matter what our circumstances are.

Suggestions:

- Teach your children that they can be happy, regardless of the circumstances.

- Remind your children that happiness is a choice; in fact, remind yourself of this occasionally.

- Remind your children to be content with the things they have been allotted. There is much happiness to be found in enjoying what we have instead of always wanting more.

- Teach your children that the secret of happiness is gratitude.

- Teach your children to smile—and smile often.

- Refrain from coveting, from envy, and from comparison—all three of these are causes of great unhappiness.

- Happiness most often comes in life as we lift and help other people. Service to others is crucial to our own happiness.

- Make sure your children get plenty of sleep and rest. They will be much happier if they have their rest.

- Limit smart phone use and social media with your children and teenagers; they will be happier.

- As a family, always have exciting things to look forward too. If you do not have anything you are looking forward to, begin to plan some exciting activities and trips.

- Forgive people who have wronged you.

- Focus on the positive aspects in life and let go of the negative.

- Exercise and spend plenty of time in outdoor activities. Children should spend a substantial amount of time outdoors.

- Spend time with friends and family. Build significant relationships with others.

- Celebrate life's victories and accomplishments.

- Clean your room and your house. Establish order in your life.

- Find the *silver lining* when you have troubles. Ask yourself questions, such as, "Is there a benefit to this challenge?" and "What can we learn from this?"

 *More on happiness*

HOLIDAYS

"Christmas: The only time of year you can sit in front of a dead tree and eat candy out of socks."
~ Anonymous[49]

Holidays have always been special to me because I can get off the merry-go-round of work and other responsibilities and focus on what is most important to me—my family. I do not know if there is a better time of year for me than that season from Thanksgiving to New Year's Day. Last year, I began listening to Christmas music in October. I could not help myself, but I needed to get my mind off politics and social issues and focus upon the things that matter most. As adults get older, being around their children during holidays is a special bonus to life. Holidays are meant for connection, rejuvenation, and laughter. Holidays have a way of strengthening relationships and bringing families and individuals together.

Suggestions:

- Have special meals that commemorate each holiday season. One of my favorite family traditions is "dinner in a pumpkin" on Halloween.

- Make your home look stunning during the Christmas holiday season. Have all of your children participate in the decorating process. If you can obtain a permit to cut a Christmas tree down in the woods, do that at least once!

- Never, never, never leave your Christmas lights up all year.

- Each Christmas, there should be several television programs and movies that become traditional in your family. Consider several, such as *How the Grinch Stole Christmas*; *It's a Wonderful Life; Miracle on 34th Street*; *A Charlie Brown Christmas*; *A Christmas Story*; *The Santa Clause*; and many others.

- Regarding gifts, a wise man advised, "Don't expect anyone to know what you want for Christmas if you don't tell them."[50]

- For Thanksgiving, make the expression of gratitude a focal point. I have celebrated Thanksgiving holidays in the past where gratitude for blessings was never mentioned—it was all about the food, and that was about it.

- To make Thanksgiving special, spend your day giving thanks to God and those who have made a difference in your life. Have your children write down their blessings on paper. Help them consider what they are grateful for and how to write messages of gratitude to others. As adults, contact several people in your life through email, text, or by phone. Let people know how grateful you are for them.

- Put an American flag in your yard to commemorate the Fourth of July, Memorial Day, Veterans Day, Flag Day, and other such occasions. Share patriotic stories and experiences with your children on those days.

- For the Fourth of July, consider attending a small-town parade, rodeo, and fireworks display.

- Holidays are time for family, friends, reflection, and gratitude.

It's hard to be a grandma without the Christmas Spirit!

 *A holiday story*

HOME IMPROVEMENT

"No trip to Home Depot is complete without at least two more trips to Home Depot for things you didn't know you would need."
~ Anonymous[51]

Every home that we have purchased has been a "fixer-upper." As a family, we have worked together as we have painted rooms, built fence, installed trim, built decks, laid tile, and hung siding. Janie and I have acquired many skills through this process, and our children have benefitted too. There is something rewarding about working on a project as a family. Perhaps even more rewarding has been observing our married children working on their own homes now. They are teaching their children how to swing a hammer and to paint a wall. As we acquire home repair skills, we are in a better position to save ourselves lots of money, but also help others.

Just recently, I was over at my son's house helping him with a project. He is now in his 30s, with a wonderful wife and five great children. My son was building a large trellis and porch swing. He had all the right tools, and his craftsmanship was much better than mine. I could not help but think back to the many home improvement projects he participated in as a kid, and I realized that those teaching moments paid off. Not only that, but the greatest satisfaction came when I saw him teaching his oldest son—my oldest grandson—how to use the tools and help in the project.

Suggestions:

- Make a list of the things you will need for a project before you go to the hardware store! There is nothing more annoying than having to visit a hardware store multiple times on the same day in order to acquire the right parts for a project.

- Own your own set of tools. Every time you go to a hardware store, buy at least one tool, and your inventory will grow over time.

- Take care of your tools and clean them often. Always put your tools back where they belong, and certainly do not leave them outside.

- Some of the basic tools most of us will need include: 1) a hammer, 2) a set of screwdrivers, 3) a set of socket wrenches, 4) an adjustable wrench, 5) a measuring tape, 6) a hand saw, 7) pliers (regular, channel lock, and needle nose), 8) a utility knife, 9) duct tape, 10) a level, and 11) goggles and gloves. Have a great place to store your tools.

- As you become more skilled, you may want to consider the following power tools: 1) a cordless drill, 2) a circular saw, 3) a miter saw or table saw, 4) a jigsaw, and 5) a power sander or belt sander.

- There are certain tools that you may only use once in a lifetime. Do not borrow those tools—rent them.

- Consider taking a free home improvement class at *Lowe's* or *Home Depot* or watching a home improvement show or *YouTube* videos to get ideas for your own home. You will want to learn some basic home repairs like unclogging a toilet, fixing a leaky faucet, hanging a light fixture, replacing an electric plug or switch, splicing a cord, installing mini-blinds, installing smoke detectors, and changing the filters in your air and heating system.

- Tap into the skillset of other people who have done home improvement projects and obtain ideas and tips from them. Work alongside them and learn their skills.

- Have access to a good handy man. You may need to hire him on occasion.

- Take *before* and *after* photographs of every home improvement project that you engage in. You will be happy that you did.

- Repaint the rooms in your home often with a new coat of paint.

- Learn how to install crown molding or trim.

- Replace the old light fixtures in your home with new and improved ones.

- Install celling fans in many of the rooms of your home.

- Learn to install tile or wood floors.

- Install a programmable thermostat.

- Add accents to the outside of your home, such as light fixtures, shutters, a vinyl fence.

HONESTY

"An honest man's the noblest work of God."
~ Alexander Pope[52]

Many years ago, we taught our young children about the principle of honesty in a family meeting. We decided to make an honesty pact—that we would all tell the truth, no matter what. Shortly after that, the Girl Scouts delivered my favorite cookies to our doorstep—Thin Mints. Since our children were anxious to eat the cookies, I determined we would use the cookies for a reward. Janie and I told each of our children that if they went to do their chores, they would all get some Girl Scout cookies. However, as our children scurried off, I became aware that one of our children was hiding behind a large recliner in our family room. I looked behind the chair and found our young three-year-old daughter, McKenzie, eating a pack of Girl Scout cook-ies! She had the box in her hands—I had caught her red handed. I said, "Kenzie, what is in your mouth?" She said, "Nothing." However, as she said, "Nothing," little chunks of cookie were flying out of her mouth. I asked her several times what was in her mouth, and she continued to tell me, "Nothing." Each time she replied, little cookie chunks were hitting me in the chest. Finally, I said, "Kenzie, why did you lie to me? We made an honesty pact—you were supposed to tell the truth." Her response was classic. She said, "I forgot." We knew as parents that teaching honesty was not going to be a one-time event.

Suggestions:

- Parents should be role models when it comes to honesty. Children should be able to believe that their parents would never lie.

- Do not cheat on your income taxes or in school. You will feel more at peace if you are honest and get a D on your test than if you cheated to obtain an A.

- Be honest in your work environment—put in a full day, plus more.

- Do not tolerate your children's lying—teach them that honesty is always the best policy and that honesty is the foundation on which trust is built. Make "honesty" a family tradition or motto.

- Keep the promises you make to others, including to your children!

- Avoid the temptation to exaggerate.

- Avoid looking for loopholes.

- If you do *not* know the facts, do not pretend as if you *do*.

- Never lie to your spouse or your children. It destroys trust. Even small white lies erode a relationship quickly.

- Compliment your children when they tell the truth and demonstrate honesty.

Just in case you are worried, Kenzie turned out to be a really great kid. She is now the mother of three children. Now, she is the one teaching her children about honesty!

 *Teaching my children the principle of honesty*

HUMILITY

"I believe the first test of a truly great man is humility."
~ John Ruskin[53]

When it comes to humility, I often think of my daughter Bethany. She never puts herself above anyone else, and she recognizes that every good thing in her life comes from God. She was the head cheerleader on her high school cheer squad. She was a great leader—but what made her great was that she was the last one to know of her greatness.

At halftime during football games, while the other cheerleaders were going to the bathroom to make sure they looked perfect, or while they talked and conversed with each other, Bethany would head up into the stands and talk to many little children—mostly young girls who wanted to be cheerleaders someday. Sometimes she would take them down on the track and teach them cheers, or just visit with them about their day.

It was fun to watch her—she was like the Pied Piper— wherever she went at a Friday Night Football game, there were always five or six little girls following her and copying every move she made. Bethany's humility allowed her to connect with everyone—old and young. As someone as beautiful as she was, and in her position as the head cheerleader, she could have been proud, conceited, and self-absorbed. However, she never was and never will be. We are all eager to learn something from someone who does not think they are better than other people.

Suggestions:

- Help your children realize that humility comes when we begin to recognize our dependence on God for everything we have. Every talent, gift, and opportunity we have comes from God. Nothing that we accomplish comes from our own doing.

- Like everything else we have talked about in this publication, if we want our children to be humble, they must see humility in their parents.

- Teach your children to serve others. This helps them recognize they are not the center of the universe.

- Teach your children to be quick to admit they are wrong. The proud person does not apologize because they think that all problems are "someone else's fault." The humble person apologizes swiftly. Encourage your children to admit their mistakes. Assure them that everyone makes mistakes and that the sooner we admit that, the better off all of us will be. If we do not learn from our mistakes, then there is no purpose in making them!

- Encourage your children to not talk about themselves excessively. In fact, the less they talk about themselves, the more humble they will be. Instead of a "me" focus, have them ask other individuals questions. Learn about others more than you gush about yourself.

- Encourage your children to be coachable, teachable, and trainable. Help them understand that to receive honest feedback from others so that they can improve is a precious gift.

- I once knew some parents who actually taught their children that they were better than everyone else was. This is not only improper, but also inappropriate. Help your children understand that they are not better than others are. Teach them that every human has special gifts and talents. In fact, teach them that they can learn from everyone—no matter their station in life.

- Teach your children to rejoice in the accomplishments of their peers. A humble person will not feel threatened by the success of their friends and family. A humble person can be happy when others succeed. Rejoice in the accomplishment of others!

- Teach your children that those who are humble listen to others.

- Teach your children to give other people the credit.

- Teach your children that instead of always going first, they can go last.

- Teach your children to ask others for advice—especially those they may believe could not help them.

- Teach your children to be open to others' suggestions, ideas, and opinions.

Bethany is still a cheerleader. However, most of her cheers are directed to her husband and her three children. I continue to admire her quiet leadership and humility.

HUMOR

"For health and the constant enjoyment of life, give me a keen
and ever present sense of humor; it is the next best thing to
an abiding faith in providence."
~ George Barrell Cheever[54]

Humor is one of the greatest gifts this life has to offer. Humor is the great medicine for stress, depression, and anxiety. My greatest goal in life is to make my children and grandchildren laugh. If on my tombstone it would say, "He made us laugh," I would feel that I accomplished everything that God needed me to do. How can anyone get through life without a healthy dose of humor?

Suggestions:

- Learn to find the humor in daily life—something funny that happens every day! Parents, try to make your children laugh often. Discover those things that will make your spouse and children laugh aloud!

- Create a culture of humor in your families. Writer Agnes Repplier said, "We cannot really love anybody with whom we never laugh."[55] Keep a file on your computer full of humorous stories, antidotes, cartoons, and social media postings. Create a file just for humorous stories.

- Share humorous stories with your family around the dinner table. Pass down humorous family stories to the next generation. Read humorous books with your children.

- Find a favorite clean comedian and listen to them often. Laughter is the best medicine—especially at the end of the day.

- Learn to use humor in your home to diffuse stressful and tense situations.

- Learn to laugh at yourselves and each other. Do not take yourselves too seriously. In addition, never direct your humor towards demeaning others.

- As I have mentioned before, write down the funny things your children say.

- Record on audio and video moments of your family members laughing—individually and collectively. That recording may come in handy one day or could simply heal the wounded soul.

Maybe my favorite thing in life is making my children laugh.

 *More on laughter*

KINDNESS

"Kindness is the essence of greatness and the fundamental characteristic of the noblest men and women I have known.
~ Joseph B. Wirthlin[56]

One of my daughters, Cassidy, is one of the kindest people I know. She is a friend to everyone. When she worked at a smoothie cafe, adults from our neighborhood would frequent that establishment often just so that Cassidy could serve them. So many people love her, and she loves them. She makes everyone feel welcome, accepted, and loved. When I am out mowing the lawn, Cassidy will often come out and bring me a glass of water. In watching Cassidy, I have come to learn that kindness is being in tune to the needs of others and then responding to these individuals with love and concern.

Suggestions:

- Teach your children to be both kind and strong. Haim Ginott, the great child psychologist, once said that there are two primary qualities we should develop in our children. He said that they should become *strong* and *humane*.[57]

- Parents, if we want our children to be kind, we must model kindness to others. Even more, we must treat our children with love, kindness, and charity.

- Share stories from your life about love, kindness, and service. Teach your children about the times that you were kind to others and when others have been kind to you. Help your children to have faith in humanity.

- Parents, this also implies that we do not judge our children harshly, criticize them, or demean them. Name-calling is forbidden; no parent should ever call their child a disparaging name.

- Teach your children that kindness begins in your own home. Discourage teasing, fighting, and all forms of contention among siblings. Encourage your children to love and serve each other.

- Help children understand that three kind gestures they can engage in is obeying their parents, participating in chores, and helping around the home. If children can do these things while not complaining, you will be successful in creating a culture of kindness in your home.

- Dr. John Gottman has taught that in order for a marriage to thrive, there should be a 5:1 ratio of positive to negative interactions between husband and wife.[58] I believe the same principle applies to family relationships. Parents should have a 5:1 ratio of positive to negative interactions with their children; and children should have a 5:1 ratio of positive to negative interactions with each other. Parents, discover ways to find the best in your children. Catch them in the act of doing something well and praise them for it. Teach them to do the same with their siblings and friends.

- In a study of healthy and effective families, researchers reported that 97 percent of successful families expressed their love to each other verbally and 94 percent expressed love by hugging.[59] Become a loving and affectionate family. In order for our children to show love, they must be loved; if we want our children to show physical affection, they must be hugged; if we want them to say kind words; we must shower them with praise; if we want our children to help and serve others, then we must help and serve them.

- Create family service projects where your family can serve others in your neighborhood and community. Try to create a culture in your family where you do more than just have fun together—you find ways to serve and help others.

- Encourage your children to do nice things for their friends and even for their peers that they do not know that well. Wishing a friend happy birthday or sending a friendly text of encouragement to a peer can go a long way.

- Teach your children that staying under the radar—or becoming stealth, if you will—is a wonderful way to demonstrate kindness. If our teens and children are taking selfies and posting them on social media as they deliver gifts to the unfortunate, many will question their motives.

- Academic studies have shown that teenagers who engage in large and small acts of kindness have increased measures of self-worth when compared to their peers who do little for others.[60]

- Take your children with you when you serve others, visit friends in the hospital, or visit those who are injured and recovering at home.

- Teach your children to be careful of being overly judgmental. Remember, there are always two sides to every story.

- Practice with your children "random acts of kindness." Along with your children, perform anonymous and loving service to others.

- Teach your children to love and serve each other.

- Teach your children to say nice things to others and to smile often.

Cassidy's smile and her happiness are contagious.

LEADERSHIP

"If you treat a man as he is, he will remain as he is, but if you treat him as if he were what he ought to be, and could be, he will become what he ought to be, and should be."
~ Gothe[61]

Most of us respond well to leaders who are kind, loving, down-to-earth, and, in some ways, unassuming. Servant leaders are the type of leaders we want to follow. These leaders roll up their sleeves and work in the trenches with their people. Such leaders are not afraid to get dirty, and they do not put themselves above anyone. We love such leaders!

One of my favorite leaders was a high school coach who inspired us. Although he was kind and loving, he expected excellence from us. We had a great relationship with him. I found that I could talk to this coach with ease. He had great skills and knowledge that he imparted to us. I later learned that he qualified for the 1976 Olympic 400 Relay Team about five years before he coached us. You know, he never mentioned that. We learned that from another coach. Because of my coach's humility and love for us, I found myself wanting to perform at my highest level. My coach inspired me to do better than I was probably capable. He got the best out of so many of us.

Another example of leadership to me has been my daughter Madison. She is the kind of leader I admire—quiet, kind, but strong and powerful. When she played high school sports, she was always as calm as a cucumber, no matter how tense or critical the situation was. She has always been the epitome of steadiness. Often, when I watched my daughter play, I was fidgeting, pacing, and stressed to the max. Yet Madison, who was actually in the game competing, was calm and composed. I always admire leaders, who, in a time of pressure or crisis, are steady and calm.

Suggestions:

As a leader, do not ever assume or give the impression that you believe you are better than those you are leading. Do not put yourself above others. Work with your people in the trenches!

- Teach your children that to lead is to serve, to build, to bless, to strengthen, to help, and to love.

- Good leaders are great teachers. They inspire others to try harder and reach higher.

- Connect and build relationships with those you lead. Without connection, you cannot lead.

- Good leaders are good listeners. Show those whom you lead that you are interested in them and that you care about them! Do this by listening!

- As a leader, be positive, kind, and optimistic. No one wants to follow a leader who is negative or critical. Always look for the good and communicate positivity to others! Try to be a leader who projects positive energy.

- Communicate constantly and clearly to those you are leading. People can follow a leader only if they know what is going on! Communicate expectations clearly.

- Become creative; think outside the box. Break tradition and create tradition. Just because something has been done for ages one way does not necessarily mean that is the right way or even the best way of doing it.

- You lead by example, by rolling your sleeves up and getting things done. Do not ever ask anyone to do anything that you are not willing to do as the leader. Leaders have to lead by example!

- Good leaders provide a vision and a way to make things happen. Good leaders should have goals and should always be working towards them.

- As a manager or boss, hire people who have skills you do not have, who know things you do not know, and who are, in many cases, smarter than you are. Moreover, do not be afraid to hire people who think differently than you do and who have differing opinions.

- As a leader, surround yourself with other great leaders. Know your limitations as a human and appoint leaders around you who have skills you do not have. Trust in the leaders you have appointed to make good decisions and get things done.

- Learn to delegate. Giving responsibilities to others, including your children, will help them grow and develop into strong leaders.

- When conducting meetings, always start them on time—even if there are only two people present.

- Keep calm in a crisis, be patient, and face your fears head on! Model steadiness and consistency, no matter how challenging the environment becomes.

- Good leaders are always open to new ideas.

- The best leaders make everyone around them better leaders. Michael Jordan made every member of the Chicago Bulls better. If there was no Michael Jordan, then Scotty Pippen would not have gone to the Hall of Fame and Steve Kerr would not have coached the Golden State Warriors to championships.

- As a leader, always seek for the counsel and input of others. Leaders must tap into the strength and collective wisdom of those around them.

- It is never a bad idea to keep a small notebook or 3x5 card close to you at all times. When ideas strike, which sometimes could be the middle of the night, write down the inspiration you are receiving and then find ways to act upon those thoughts and ideas that have come to you.

I am proud of my son, Brandon, for not only being a vocal leader but also backing up his words with his own actions. As a leader on his teams, he did not mind challenging his teammates and correcting them if they needed it. He expected the same treatment from them.

 *What good leaders do*

MAINTAINING A HOUSEHOLD

"Order means light and peace,
inward liberty and free command over
one's self; order is power."
~ Henri Frederic Amiel[62]

I remember, years ago, walking into a fellow Church member's home in Centralia, Washington. Since I grew up in a relatively clean home, I could not believe what I saw. The entire home looked like it had been ransacked or vandalized. There literally was not a square inch of the floor that was free of debris, toys, clothes, or other clutter. Every piece of furniture in their home was equally covered with clothes, toys, dirty diapers, and other forms of squalor. After a short visit with this family, we left their home and wondered if this young family lived in this manner each day, or if we just happened to catch them at a bad time—like right after a riot had ensued at their home. However, I had the occasion of going back to their home on several occasions, and each time it looked relatively the same—toys strewn all over the floor, clothes spread out everywhere, dirty dishes in the family room, fossilized baby bottles with hardened formula in them laying on couches. Nope! It was not a fluke. This is how the family lived. Since the man was a leader in our Church, I found myself in shock that he and his wife chose to live this way.

I contrast this experience with many others I have had over the years when I have entered into a pristine, clean home. I have learned that a special spirit and feeling occupies such homes. These are homes that do not necessarily look like palaces, but in many ways, they feel that way. The carpets are vacuumed, the tile is clean, and the rooms are clean and tidy. Often, there is wonderful artwork on the walls, soft music playing in the background, spaces to sit and relax, and inviting food to eat.

I love when I come home after a hard day of work and walk into such a wonderful, clean home and sit with my wife, Janie. Such a home gives me a sense of order in this world and certainly makes me feel like my home is a refuge from the storms of life. To me, nothing is better than a clean home, a stocked refrigerator, some instrumental music playing in the background, and my family close by. However, a home without my family is merely a house.

Suggestions:

- Have a special place in your home for everything. Have a place for car keys, phones, wallets, purses, and other things that are easy to misplace. At the end of each day, make sure everything is in its proper place, such as papers, homework, backpacks, glasses, headphones, DVDs, plates, knives, cups, bowls, spoons, remote controls, blankets, and anything else that may be used frequently in your home. As Benjamin Franklin said, "A place for everything, everything in its place."[63]

- Have a designated day each week on which you clean your home thoroughly. For some reason, in our home, that was always Monday.

- Make sure bathrooms, including toilets, are cleaned thoroughly at least weekly, if not more often.

- Kitchens should be cleaned daily.

- Mop and vacuum floors often.

- Maintaining a household with children takes constant effort. You cannot clean your home once a week and think that is enough. Children can mess things up quickly. Each day in a home with children should be spent having fun, playing, messing things up, and then cleaning things up.

- I recommend that you never go to bed with a dirty home or with dishes in the sink. Wake up to a clean home every day.

- Learn to do your laundry appropriately, and teach your children to eventually wash, dry, and sort their own clothing.

- Learn to prepare food and make practical meals. Learn to meal plan so that you can purchase food for meals in advance.

- Maintain a grocery list.

- Recycle.

- Have a file or a drawer to keep and sort mail, bills, children's papers, medical documents, and other important records.

- Keep a list of the items around your home that need to be fixed or repaired. Chip away at this list constantly.

- Create routines and schedules for your family, and follow your program closely.

- Clean out your garage on a regular basis.

- Get rid of the debris and junk in your life by hauling things off regularly to Goodwill, the Salvation Army, Deseret Industries, or the local landfill.

- Learn how to declutter your home spaces—less is often more.

- Learn to live off a budget to build savings and prepare for a "rainy day," or for fun trips and special events.

MARKS OF MATURITY

"If we want our kids to have a shot at making it in the world as eighteen-year-olds, with the umbilical cord of the cell phone being their go-to solution in all manner of things, they're going to need a set of basic life skills."
~ Julie Lythcott-Haims[64]

Several years ago, I was talking to another parent about our college-aged children. We were discussing whether our children would be flying or driving home from their university studies for the Christmas holidays—roughly, a 1200-mile trip from Utah to Texas. During our conversation, this parent said to me, "Well, what can we do? Our children are adults now, so we have no say." I thought to myself, "Adults? What do you mean 'adults'"? In my mind, even though my child was over twenty-years of age, I did not consider them an adult. I was paying for their tuition and books. In fact, I was paying for most of their housing. I was even paying for the trip for them to come home! I helped them purchase their car and was paying for the insurance. And they were certainly on my cell phone plan. It was my belief that once children become financially independent from their parents, then we can begin discussing adulthood. However, there is much more to adulthood than mere financial independence—but that is a wonderful starting place!

Not long after this experience, I was visiting with some friends at a wedding reception. As I was conversing with the mother of the groom, she confided in me, "I just don't know how we are going to afford to have a married son." I was curious about that comment. Although Janie and I did not have any married children at that time, I assumed that when your children "left the nest," life would become less expensive—not more. The mother then explained that they would be paying the $800-a-month rent for their son and his new bride, along with their car insurance and cell phones. Then she gave the line that I had heard before, "But, since they are adults, we really cannot say anything about the arrangement." Since when did this become a rule—that you cannot talk to "adults" who live off your hard-earned income? That was news to me. I would not classify this newlywed couple as adults—but that's just me.

In my own opinion, here are some great maturity indicators:

Hardworking	Responsible
Humble	Flexible
Able to resolve conflict in a healthy manner	Driven
Able to make sacrifices	Able to delay gratification
Can have conversations with adults	Can put the needs of others before their own
Shows gratitude to others	Self-disciplined
Patient	Strives to make wise decisions

| Produces more than they consume | Priorities are centered on adult-like choices |

Suggestions:

- Adults should be able to strike up conversations with strangers and those they do not know that well.

- Adults should be able to find their way around their local neighborhoods, communities, cities, and universities. In fact, adults should be able to travel by air or land on their own, without the help of others.

- Adults must manage their assignments, workloads, and deadlines, without the help of others.

- Adults should be able to wake up early and go to bed at a decent hour.

- Adults should be able to clean up after themselves, construct their environments with some form of order, and manage their households. Adults should be able to solve their own problems—especially problems with other people.

- Adults should be able to cope with the difficulties and challenges of life.

- Adults should be able to earn money, manage money, and budget money.

- Adults should be able to live independently of others.

- Adults should be able to control their passions, their emotions, their drives, and their temper.

- Adults can stand up for what they believe in.

- Adults can try to understand an opposing viewpoint.

- Adults are not egocentric—they know they are a small cog in a mighty machine.

- Adults can forgive others.

- Adults should be able to do hard things. Hence, adults should be resilient and have some grit.[65]

More on marks of maturity

MANNERS

"Nothing is more reasonable and cheap than good manners."
~ Anonymous[66]

As our children got older and began participating in organized sports, I often elected to help coach their teams. This meant two things: 1) my children would usually get to start at their positions, and 2) I ended up driving several players home from practice a couple of times each week. It did not take long for me to determine which of our players came from strong homes and which ones did not. The test was easy. It was a simple "thanks for the ride" test. When we dropped children off at their homes, and they said, "Thanks for the ride," that was all I needed to know about them and their parents. Not all children did this; in fact, many never expressed a word of thanks. I took that as a lesson, and we drilled it into our children that they always needed to say "thank you" when they were given treats by their coaches and/or team mothers, and when they were given rides home. I hope my children will pass this legacy down to the next generation.

Suggestions:

- The words "please" and "thank you" should be taught at an early age.

- When people ask you how you how you are doing, tell them how wonderful you feel, and how great life is—even if it is not! Be positive, not negative. And then, ask them how they are doing.

- Teach your sons to always give girls or women their chairs when there are none left in the room. The same rule applies to older people. If you are riding on a shuttle bus to an airport, and there are women and senior citizens standing in the aisles, give them your seat.

- Make sure that your children are the ones in your community who always express thanks to those who drove them somewhere; "Thanks for the ride!" is a simple expression.

- Create a culture in your home of being "mannerly" to each other. Many children say "please" and "thank you" to others but sometimes do not treat their family members with the same expressions. Husbands and wives would also do well to express kindnesses to each other.

- Teach your children to share and to take turns.

- Be punctual to family and community events you attend. If a family dinner begins at 5:00 p.m., show up a few minutes early and ask what you can do to help. Too many people show up to events five minutes late, not realizing that someone else had to arrive 15 minutes early to set up the chairs and prepare the room.

- To help your children understand what manners are, occasionally point out an example of someone demonstrating "bad" manners or "no" manners.

- Teach your children that they should not interrupt others when they are talking.

- Help your children develop social skills and interact with others. Teach your children to compliment and praise their friends and associates. Teach them this skill by praising them often.

- Teach your children to respect adults, to treat them with kindness, and to never assume that they know more than adults, such as teachers, coaches, administers, church leaders, and other authority figures.

- Teach your children to keep their negative, or even their strong, opinions to themselves. Most people are not interested in our negative, judgmental, or harsh opinions.

- Always compliment the person who cooked the meal, whether that be in your own home or in the home of someone else. Indeed, compliment the chef!

- Teach your children to ask for permission rather than forgiveness.

- Teach your children to never make fun of anyone else.

- Teach your children that when someone is working on something, engaged in a project, or carrying a heavy load, simply ask, "Can I help?"

- Teach your children to not all talk at once, but to speak

one person at a time.

- Teach your children to cover their mouth/nose when they cough or sneeze.

- Teach them to send a thank-you note, or even a thank-you text, when someone does something for them.

- Teach your children to hold the door open for other people.

- Teach your children to shake hands firmly and to look people in the eye when they speak to them.

- Treat the janitor and the lawn crew as well as you would royalty.

- Never ask someone to babysit your children for a long period of time if they are not potty trained, and if they do not sleep through the night.

- Never ask someone to babysit your children if they are sick.

- Do not ask anyone to babysit your children on a holiday. A family in our neighborhood once asked us to watch their children over the Christmas holidays while they traveled Europe. Not cool!

- Never ask someone to do something for your children that you are not willing to do.

- Do not correct or discipline other people's children, even if you are related. It is not your place to correct other people's children, unless a child is in immediate danger!

MARRIAGE

"Think the best of each other, especially of those, you say you love. Assume the good and doubt the bad."
~ Jeffrey R. Holland[67]

I remember once driving in the car on a Saturday afternoon with my wife, Janie. While running errands, we became stuck in some healthy Dallas traffic. In fact, it seemed that we were sitting at a stop light for ten full minutes. Being the most impatient person I know, I finagled my way out of one lane, across another, and then took a dirt road short cut behind a strip mall. As we were bouncing through potholes but making great time, I looked at my wife and asked, "Honey, how many field trips have I taken you on throughout our life?" With her dry wit that she inherited from her father, she looked at me and said, "Figuratively, or literally?" I was not sure it was safe to respond to either of those options.

Suggestions:

- When it comes to marriage, your first focal point should be, first, to find the right person. Second, once you have found the right person, you should strive to become the right person for them. Once you have done these two things, do all in your power to make the relationship successful. More effort should be directed towards your marriage than your job, your children, or your hobbies. Remember, choose your love, then, for the rest of your life, you are to love your choice!

- Teach your children to never marry anyone because of fear, and certainly, teach them not to marry someone whom they think they can change.

- Go on a weekly date with your spouse. Take turns planning the dates. Make it a regular and consistent program—every Friday night or Saturday night. Also, consider when your teenagers are busy with their activities, lunch dates are another good option—your Fridays and Saturdays may be consumed with parenting obligations. Remember: babysitters are cheaper than divorces. In fact, once you find a good babysitter, do everything in your power to keep them happy!

- Do not ever become apathetic in your marriage. You must constantly keep the spark alive. Find ways to do that!

- Live by the 7-7-7 rule. Every seven days, you go on a date. Every seven weeks, you go on an overnight retreat. Every seven years, you go on a cruise.

- Together, read the book, *His Needs, Her Needs* by Willard Harley. Find out what your spouse's needs are and try to meet them often.

- Have a weekly meeting with your spouse where you can coordinate schedules, plan dates, discuss the budget, and discuss the needs of your family. Set goals with your spouse and review them often. These goals should center on marriage and family life. When you dream, dream big and bold!

- Develop a hobby together.

- Dance together, especially when no one is watching.

- Express gratitude and appreciation to your spouse often. Write love letters to your spouse and surprise them with fun and exciting things.

- Connect with your spouse physically each day. Demonstrate some kind of daily physical affection.

- Show affection to each other in front of the children. Let there be no doubt in your children's mind that their parents are crazy about each other.

- Always build your spouse up in front of others.

- Together with your spouse, read the book, *The Five Love Languages* by Gary Chapman. Discover your spouse's primary and secondary love language and try to speak through that language each day.

- Find ways to serve and help your spouse on a regular basis. I once heard marriage expert, Dr. Douglas Brinley, say, "No husband has ever been shot by his wife while doing the dishes!"

- Find ways to connect with your spouse daily by going

on walks, talking on the phone, texting, and doing other things to spend time together.

- Remember: your spouse comes before your children.

- Create projects around your home and community where you and your spouse can work together as a team.

- Read parenting books together on a regular basis. Create a parenting belief system and strategy. Have a deliberate plan when it comes to raising your children—do not leave something so important to chance!

- When you fight or argue as a couple, keep it between yourselves. If you tell other people your problems, they will remember them, and you will eventually move past those problems. Yet, those you have shared your problems with will assume you are still dealing with those things.

- Strive to place your spouse's needs before your own.

- Forgive your spouse quickly and seek forgiveness from them. Be swift to apologize.

- Focus on each other's strengths and learn to ignore each other's weaknesses.

- Find reasons to laugh together often.

MENTAL AND EMOTIONAL STRENGTH

*"Instead of preparing children to deal with the inevitable
scratches, bumps, and bruises of growing up, [modern parents]
insist that we should swaddle them in bubble wrap…
A child raised in a bubble wrap is not prepared
for the symptoms of life."*
~ Charles J. Sykes[68]

It was always enjoyable for me to drive home with my children after their high school games. When they won, we celebrated and talked about many of the good things they did during the game. When they lost, we did the same thing—we focused on the good. I wanted to stay positive with them. A few days later, when they were ready and open, we could discuss some of the things they could have done better. I always believed that my children could learn much more about themselves, and about life, from their losses rather than their wins. They just had to be in the right frame of mind to receive those lessons. Most often, they were able to get into that space. Sometimes it took half a pizza and a bowl of coco puffs to get them to that point, and that was all right by me.

Suggestions:

- Teach your children to deal with both good and bad experiences. They can learn lessons from failures and losses perhaps even more than from their successes. Help them understand that bad things happen to good people. Teach them that disappointment and failure is how we learn to cope and deal with the real world.

- As parents, stand for principles, values, and your beliefs. Do not waver when it comes to your standards. This world needs more people who are willing to stand up and be counted. Teach your children to do the same.

- Teach your children to be leaders and not followers. Following the crowd is one of the easiest things a human can do. What is challenging, and becoming more difficult all of the time, is to stand up for what is right—which often means standing alone. If they choose to lead, others will be willing to follow.

- Inspire your children with stories from the scriptures, like those of Daniel, David, Esther, Jesus, and others where people stood tall and strong in the face of tremendous opposition. Inspire them with stories where people stood strong and tall from American history, sports, your own personal life, and from the lives of family members.

- Help your children identify the family standards, rules, principles, and religious beliefs that you will adhere to—no matter what.

- Engage in role-plays in your home when you can teach your children how to stand up for their beliefs. Demonstrate to them how to decline an offer to take drugs or engage in sexual behavior. Teach them the "hows" and even the "whys"!

- Teach your children that they will be more equipped to stay strong and resist negative peer pressure if they have like-minded friends. There is great strength in numbers. If they choose friends with similar values, they can strengthen and encourage each other.

- Parents, share experiences from your own life where you had to take a stand. Let your children know about the experiences where you had to stand alone or where you had to stand up in the face of strong opposition.

- Encourage your children to look for heroes in their lives—people whom they can look to and admire. Specifically, point them to individuals who have stood up for the right. Be a hero to your children.

- Teach your children to set a proper example that others will want to follow. Teach them to be brave, to work hard, and to be kind to others. There will always be those who will want to follow them.

I loved watching my children venture into new areas, and try new things. I never dreamed three of my girls would be pole-vaulters, and neither did they.

NEIGHBORHOODS

"I've always wanted to have a neighbor just like you. I've always wanted to live in a neighborhood with you."
~ Fred Rogers[69]

I do miss the good ole' days when neighbors loved each other, talked to each other, and associated together. We had a neighborhood like that in San Antonio, Texas many years ago. Everyone knew each other, people helped each other, and neighbors took care of each other. I loved our block parties and have fond memories of neighbors out on their yards in the evening, talking to each other.

Many years later, we raised our children in the Dallas area. We lived in the same neighborhood for over ten years. The day we packed up our moving truck to leave, not one person on our street even noticed we were leaving. In that neighborhood, no one really talked to each other or associated together. It was a sad commentary on how our world has become more isolated and self-absorbed. Perhaps we could have done more to make that neighborhood a better place.

Suggestions:

- Take the initiative when it comes to getting to know your neighbors. Introduce yourself to your neighbors—do not expect them to make the first move.

- Serve your neighbors. Be willing to get your neighbor's mail and watch their home when they are away on vacation. Shovel the snow off your neighbor's walks, rake their leaves, or do other service for them.

- Get to know your neighbors by inviting them over for dinners, barbeques, and activities.

- Be the instigator in having annual block parties with your neighbors.

- Bring treats to your neighbors on holidays and special occasions.

- Take pride in the way your neighborhood looks. Occasionally take your family through your neighborhood and pick up garbage on the side of the road or in people's yards.

- Be friendly and wave to your neighbors as you drive by their homes. Be the first to say hello.

- Be courteous to your neighbors by not parking your car in front of their home, making excessive noise, or having a messy lawn or home appearance. Ensure that your home has a healthy dose of curb appeal.

- Do not ever be that neighbor whose dogs bark incessantly all day and night and poop in other neighbors' yards.

- Handle conflicts with neighbors in kind and respectful ways.

- Communicate with your neighbors, share key information with them, and keep them in the loop.

More on neighborhoods and communities

PARENTING TODDLERS

"When we give children our own time, we are giving them our presence, a gift that is always noticed"
~ Spencer W. Kimball[70]

One thing that I remember about when our children were young—especially when they were learning how to talk—was the hilarious things they would say. I remember once, the night before Easter morning, we were saying evening prayers with our children. My three-year-old son said, "Dear Heavenly Father, we are thankful that the Easter Bunny died for our sins." My wife and I looked at each other and knew that we needed more work on Bible stories in our home. My children have said so many funny things over the years, and now my grandchildren are saying them. My mistake: I did not write most of them down. Learn from my mistake.

Suggestions:

- Ask your parents and in-laws as much as you can about how to be a successful parent. We can learn something from even the worst parents, albeit not that much.

- Also, do not ever shy away from identifying a couple in

your neighborhood or community that you can look up to and respect as parents. Ask them questions about child rearing and about their parenting beliefs and philosophies. Identify someone in your life who is a role model when it comes to parenting and strive to emulate them. In my counseling practice, I see too many young married couples today who are not seeking out parenting mentors. Instead, they turn to books or to the internet to learn parenting skills—often from authors and experts who do not have children. Seek to have a dialogue with someone who has been down the path you are traversing.

- Do not compare your toddler to what other toddlers are doing at their age. Who cares whose teeth came in first or who can crawl the fastest? Spend more time enjoying your child rather than comparing them to the neighbor's "Savant."

- Read daily to your toddler. Even though they may not comprehend what is being said, this will serve as a foundation for their education, help them develop verbal and intellectual skills, and propel them on the road to academic success.

- Sleep-train your baby. It may take several nights of them crying all night long, but the results are incredible. If you can get them going to sleep in the early evening, you and your spouse can have some time to yourselves to reconnect and relax after a long day.

- Avoid the temptation to let your toddler sleep with you in your bed.

- As your toddler begins to talk, write down the funny things they say from age 18 months to 18 years. This is something I wish I had done with my children.

- Both mothers and fathers should have "playtime" with their toddler often. Take your toddler for walks or even jogs in their stroller regularly. Train them early to love the outdoors.

- If you toddler is in pain, like with an ear infection, give them some pain medication. If your eardrum felt like it was about to burst, I promise you would be pumping pain meds through an IV drip. I frequently see parents who will not give their children pain relief until it is convenient for them.

- Snuggle with your toddler often and show them tons of physical affection.

- Find ways to extinguish temper tantrums quickly. When your child has a meltdown in the store because you did not buy them something, do not solve the problem by going to buy them something!

- Learn to ignore some of the annoying things your toddler does.

- Keep a daily schedule and routine with your toddlers. Help make the world predictable.

- Use natural and logical consequences to teach your toddler appropriate behavior.

 *A story about parenting toddlers*

PARENTING CHILDREN

"Every child should spend a substantial amount of time with somebody who's crazy about him or her...There has to be at least one person who has an irrational involvement with that child, someone who thinks that kid is more important that other people's kids, someone who's in love him or her, and whom he or she loves in return...You can't pay a [person] to do what a [parent] will do for free."
~ Dr. Urie Brofenbrenner[71]

I remember one time when our children did something that Janie and I did not appreciate. Fortunately, I cannot remember what they did wrong. I do remember gathering them in our family room. At the time, most of them would have been in elementary school. I was trying to make the point that they seemed somewhat ungrateful. I said, "Do you all understand that we give you everything?! We give you the clothes you wear, the food you eat, and even the air you breathe! (Which was quite an exaggeration, but I was a bit riled up.) Our daughter Bethany, who was probably in third grade at the time, and who was our calmest kid by far, came back with, "Oh yea, well you're not going to take this breath." Then she took a bite of the air. I have no idea what that meant, and it was uncharacteristic of her to talk that way, but her act of rebellion caused us all to laugh hysterically and forget about what our children had done wrong in the first place.

Suggestions:

- Express love to your children often. Shower them with kind words, physical affection, and time together. The most important thing you can do with your children is to develop a relationship with them. If you do not have a relationship, you cannot influence or teach them.

- Regulate your children. This is so crucial when they are young. Designate a time for them to go to bed and wake up—children need routine. By the time they are three, they could do a household chore or two. Research shows that children who are regulated in childhood learn to self-regulate as adolescents and adults.[72]

- After you correct, punish, or discipline your children, make sure you go back to them and show them an abundance of love. Hug them and let them know you care about them.

- Be at the crossroads for your children. Find time to be involved in their lives. Have a snack and some good connection time each day when your children come home from school.

- Establish an incredible nighttime routine with your children, complete with a snack, a story, taking to them, and tucking them in bed. This may take some effort, but the dividends will pay off for years to come. Do not let your child/children sleep with you in your bed. Once you open that door, it becomes very difficult to close.

- Have fun with your children. Jump with them on your trampoline; swing with them in the park; play kickball and soccer with them. Listen to music with your children. Sing and dance while you work together.

- Encourage your children to participate in a sport. Some of life's greatest lessons can be learned on the playing field. If your schedule allows it, coach your children's teams. This could be a great bonding experience and a great excuse to spend time with your children. Make it a positive experience.

- Help your children to be physically active. Exercise and engage in outdoor activities with them. Ride bikes and swim with your children. Take your children hiking and camping.

- Consider getting a pet for your children to take care of. Taking care of animals can help them become more compassionate, kind, and loving. If you do not get an animal, take your children to feed animals—horses and goats, for example—often.

- Encourage your children to play a musical instrument or at least engage in a cultural activity. Music can bless their lives in many ways and increase their academic performance.

- Be involved with your children's education. Attend parent/teacher conferences. Help your children with their homework. Read to your children often. Find ways to teach your children values through the books and scriptures you choose to read to them.

- Read with your children often.

- If you have several children, find ways to spend individual time with each child. Take your children to do things that they enjoy doing.

- Make sure your children have chores and responsibilities.

- Teach your children how to solve their own problems and how to do things on their own.

- Teach your children key manners—especially to say *please* and *thank you.*

- Let your children talk while you practice being a fantastic listener.

- Teach your children how to manage money at a young age.

- Set goals with your children.

- Praise your children more than you correct them.

- Never be the kind of parent who believes that your children can do nothing wrong.

I miss the days when our children were just little kids. Yes, it was tiring, and yes, it was exhausting. However, I miss the days of watching them play together, listening to them giggle, watching them use their imaginations. I miss looking out the back window and watching them play for hours together in our back yard and remembering what it was like not to have a care in the world.

 *Parenting lessons gone south*

PARENTING TEENAGERS

"Rules without relationship equals rebellion"
~ Anonymous[73]

Speaking of Bethany, I remember another occasion many years later. Bethany was now a senior in high school and the head cheerleader on the varsity squad. On a Saturday afternoon, we were cleaning our garage and getting rid of some old stuff. Bethany went with me as we hauled a trailer load of junk to the dump. As I watched my daughter tossing things out of our trailer into a big heap of mess, I thought to myself, "How many high school cheerleaders in America are at a dump today with their dads?" I concluded that there probably were not many. My heart swelled with love as I realized that I had a strong enough relationship with my daughter that she would want to be with me, doing such menial work. Of course, I also remembered that I promised her a Slurpee on our way home, so that may have also had something to do with our bonding experience that day.

Suggestions:

- Consider a "no spend the night" rule with your children. As a parent, I have learned that there is not much good that happens when children spend the night or sleep over with their peers.

- Teach your teenagers to work by working with them.

- Find hobbies that you can enjoy with your teens.

- All teenage children need three things: *1) connection, 2) regulation,* and *3) autonomy*. Find ways with each individual child in your family to make these three things happen.

- *Connect with your children*. Find things that you can do with them to build a strong and lasting relationship.

- *Regulate your children*: They need chores, rules, and responsibilities. They should have a curfew—and you should always know where they are. Take away privileges if adolescents cannot handle the freedom you have given them. Moreover, give them more freedom and privileges when they prove, by their actions, that they can be trusted.

- *Give your children some autonomy*: Give them an opportunity to develop some of their own ideas and ways of doing things. Listen to their opinions respectfully and help them discover why they feel the way that they do. A great question for teenagers is, "So, how do you feel about that?"

- Come to know your teenagers' friends. During this critical time of life, friends can make or break your children.

- Regulate all media use with your adolescents. Do not buy them smart phones until they are old enough to handle them. Regulate their computer time. Television watching should be limited and monitored as well. Keep close tabs on video game content and how long they are allowed to play. Minimize their time with video games, social media, and other electronics.

- Consider keeping your teens' cell phones out of their rooms. Teens should not be sleeping with their cell phones. Do not buy into the argument that their phone is their alarm clock. You can buy them a $5.00 alarm clock at Walmart. In my opinion, teens' phones should be turned into their parents or a neutral location each night before bed.

- In the most-used room of your home, have a basket for cell phones—make it a *no-phone-zone*. Spend time talking and building relationships with your family.

- Do not allow your children to view movies or television programs with sexual content. Furthermore, be cautious of the violence they are exposed to in movies and television.

- Resist the temptation to buy your teen a brand-new car—a used car is just fine. Encourage them to be responsible by purchasing some gas and keeping the car clean.

- Pay close attention to whom your children date. Discourage steady dating until children are older, more mature, and can handle the powerful emotions that dating brings.

- Have the courage to talk to your teenagers about difficult topics like sexual relationships, intimacy, mental health issues, religion, and politics.

- Be friends with your teenagers' friends and their parents. Have your children's friends over to your home often.

When our children were younger, parents would approach me and, in a tone of warning, say, "Wait until all of those kids become teenagers." I could not wait. I looked forward to the teenage years with great anticipation. My favorite time of life was when our children were teenagers. I would do it again if I could. I loved laughing with them, playing pranks on them, and being there for them when they had their challenges and struggles. It was not perfect, and we had our share of late-night discussions and even times of disappointment. However, looking back, it was the greatest time of life for Janie and me.

PERSONAL AND FAMILY HYGIENE

"Cleanliness is next to Godliness."
~ John Wesley[74]

We all need to take care of ourselves—washing, bathing, brushing our teeth, and so on. People will not take us seriously, no matter how bright we may appear, if we have poor hygiene. I used to work with a man who often liked to talk to me—face to face. Even though he was a sharp looking person, I never heard one word he ever said to me. All I could think of the entire time he was talking to me was, "Man, you need a mint or some breath freshener." Because his breath was so terrible, it was very difficult to take him seriously.

Another time in my counseling practice, I saw a couple that were having difficulties in their marriage. The wife was upset because her husband never wanted to be intimate with her. In one individual session, I asked the husband, "So why is it that you don't seem to have any interest in having an intimate relationship with your wife?" He said, "Do you really want to know?" I said, "Of course I do." He then said, "My wife stinks. She rarely showers, and her breath smells horrific." That was all I needed to know—made perfect sense to me!

Suggestions:

- Your babies and children should have baths or showers daily. Your children should wash their hair at least several times a week. Teach your teenagers to use deodorant, mouthwash, and perhaps a slight dab of cologne or perfume.

- Never change your baby's diaper in the busiest room of the house. When you change your baby's diaper in your home, or someone else's home, you should take the diaper to an outdoor garbage can. Do not leave the diaper on the family room floor, kitchen table, or countertop—just speaking hypothetically, of course.

- Teach your children to brush their teeth after every meal, or at least twice a day. Flossing or water pics can also be helpful for the best dental hygiene. Some experts recommend not leaving toothbrushes next to the toilet (for about 70 reasons) but instead keeping them in a more ventilated, protected area.

- If you can afford it, have your children's crooked teeth straightened, have their chipped tooth repaired, and have their dull-colored teeth whitened.

- Teach your children to brush and comb their own hair.

- Teach your children to wash their hands after using the rest room and after being in public places. While you are teaching them, you may want to wash up as well.

- If you have a kid with stinky feet, help them out, for goodness' sake! Teach them proper foot care and hygiene.

- Adults and children should always wash their hands with soap before preparing meals or eating food.

- Teach your children to cover their nose and mouth when they cough or sneeze. Today, the new trend is to cough or sneeze into your elbow, arm, or shirt. Those are not my favorite options, but then again, no one asked me.

- When a child is sick, make sure you spray your home with sanitizer, and clean the area where they were resting. Keep them home on such days—do not send them into public places to spread their germs. Keep them home from school and other activities if they are sick. Keep them away from other friends or family during those sick times. Too many parents today expose their sick children to others—definitely not cool!

- Teach your children to make their bed daily and change their sheets weekly.

- After each meal, teach your children to rinse off their plate and silverware and then to place them in the dishwasher. One wise man counseled, "Never go to bed with dirty dishes in the sink."[75]

 *Practicing Good Hygiene*

RESILIENCE

"A child cannot possibly develop resilience when his parents are constantly at his side, interfering with the development of autonomy, self-management, and coping skills."
~ Dr. Madeline Levine[76]

I remember when our daughter Callie had to make a monumental decision. She had been a cheerleader most of her life, but because of some drama, conflict, and personality issues on the cheer squad, she decided, going into her senior year in high school, that she no longer needed cheerleading. Instead, she took up the sport of cross-country running. Although she did not set any school records, she loved running. In fact, she continues to run competitively as an adult. I know how difficult it was for her to leave the popularity and status that came with cheerleading. She practically had to retool her entire identity. However, she made it.

Our daughter, Natalie, lost a school election. As her dad, it was devastating to watch her experience that difficult trial. However, the next year, she ran again and won. I loved that she never gave up. Her senior year she broke her hand during a practice the first week of the season. She ended up missing most of her senior year, but she never complained. She just muscled through it.

Cassidy moved with us just before her sophomore year in high school. Moving from Texas to Utah was most difficult for her. She left her social life and friends for a life of some loneliness and uncertainly. However, she weathered the storm and rose above those challenges. By her senior year, she was the president of her choir, starred in a play, and had made several wonderful friends. I love watching my children demonstrate resilience.

Suggestions:

- In order to teach resilience, parents must be resilient!

- As a parent, do not solve all of your children's problems— help give them the tools to solve their own problems!

- Teach your children the virtue of toughness. They will need coping skills to deal with the crazy world they will live in. Coddling them and hovering over them will not make them into mature, responsible adults. Teach them that they can do hard things! Share with them your own personal triumphs and stories of resiliency.

- Teach children to tolerate some discomfort. Not everything they do in this world will be like a ride at Disneyland. Many things in life are hard; other things are downright painful.

- Encourage your children to solve their own problems

when possible and to take some reasonable risks. Do not try to meet every need your children have. They may have to go without some of the items on their "wish list."

- Allow your children to fail. Teach them natural and logical consequences. If they forgot to bring their lunch to school, resist the temptation to bring their lunch to them. Going hungry for one meal can be an eloquent sermon. Hara Marano wrote, "A child who never experiences failure will view anything less than total success as failure. A wholly sanitized childhood will only defer failure until later."[77]

- When your children mess up, make mistakes, or fail a test, connect with them by sharing some of your own failures and disappointments in life. Do your children know those stories?

- Teach your children that losing is part of life. Not everyone will become the student body president, become first chair in the band, or be the starting quarterback on the football team. Although we do not want to make a habit of losing, there are great lessons that can be learned when life does not go as planned. Help your children learn those lessons, be tough, and bounce back. Some of the greatest sermons every preached emerge from losses and setbacks.

- Teach your children how to stretch, grow, and get out of their comfort zones.

- Teach your children to bounce back after experiencing tough times.

- Teach your children how to manage their emotions. Children and teens do not need to cry or whine every time they do not get their way.

- Encourage your children to try new things—even if that is as simple as trying a new food at a restaurant. Help them build skills in talents in areas they never have thought of before.

- Give your children increasing responsibility for managing their own lives. Have them set their own alarm clock and wake up by themselves. Teach them to work hard in order to pay for some of their essentials, like clothes, cell phones, tuition for college, and even gas for the car they drive.

- Help your children process and learn from the consequences of their behaviors.

- Help your children maintain a positive attitude when there is crisis or chaos around them. Help them to be optimistic and see the good.

- Teach your children to delay or postpone gratification.

- Do not feel that as a parent, you need to give your child all of the answers. Let them wrestle with their problems and help provide them with the tools to find answers on their own.

- Show your children how to face their fears.

- Give your children responsibilities.

- Hold your children accountable.

- Teach your children to avoid the "victim mentality." Teach them to act and not be acted upon!

- Help your children develop incredible life skills, such as social skills, problem solving, and mental toughness.

- Teach them to move on! Get past the issue. Let it go and move forward.

Natalie missed most of her senior volleyball season due to a broken hand, but, hey, at least she got a great photo just before the season began!

Callie transitioned from cheerleading to running. Since then, she has never looked back. I proud of this girl and her iron will and resilient spirit.

SELF-NURTURING

"Take time to do what makes your soul happy."
~ Unknown[78]

Self-nurturing is an area of my life where I need improvement. Years ago, when we lived in Dallas, we had a major ice storm, and almost everything in town shut down for the day. In fact, each of our teenagers had activities that night—and, one by one—each of those activities were cancelled. For the first time in many months, our family had a free night with nothing to do. A free night! I knew exactly what we could do! I went over to the grocery store and rented a carpet cleaner, and we steam-cleaned our carpets that night. A few days later, I was talking to a friend. He said, "Wasn't last Wednesday night great—just a free night home with the family!" I asked, "What did you all do on your 'free night?'" He said, "You know, we made hot chocolate and sat by the fireplace and just talked. And then we watched a movie together as a family." I was so embarrassed that I had our family clean the carpets that I did not have the guts to tell him what we did on our "free night." However, that was the point I realized that I needed some therapy. The thought of relaxing or watching a movie never occurred to me.

Here is another true confession. I tend to think that you have to get away from the hustle and bustle of life in order to relax. Several years ago, a neighbor invited our family to a barbeque at their home. They had a swimming pool that made their backyard much more fun than our own. We were to be at their home on a Saturday afternoon at 4:00 p.m. After some professional work I had to do in the morning, we gathered the kids together to get some indoor chores done. Then, we cleaned the garage, took a load of things to the dump—and to Goodwill—and then got the lawn mowed. We were scrambling to get our "to-do-list" taken care so that we could eventually enjoy the day. However, when we finally arrived at our neighbor's house, it was as if we had entered another world. There, in his backyard, my friend was sitting in a recliner by his pool, listening to jazz music and reading a book. It was as if he did not have a care in the world. As I looked at him, I thought, "Okay, when I grow up—I want to be you!" I realized in my life, relaxing was something that I never made time for, and I needed to build that into my world. I am still working on that.

Suggestions:

- Too many of us spend so much time helping and serving others that we neglect our own physical and mental health; take some time for yourself each day. In Stephen R. Covey's book, *The Seven Habits of Highly Effective People*, habit seven is to "sharpen the saw."[79] If we continually saw, the blade will become dull. Therefore, taking time to sharpen the saw in your own life is to renew yourself physically, spiritually, mentally, and so-cially/emotionally.

- Take bubble baths often; and while doing so, listen to some awesome, relaxing music.

- Get a neck massager and use it regularly.

- Invest in a nice foot massager. It may cost you some money, but the results will exceed the cost.

- Consider investing in a nice massage chair.

- Download the "Calm" or "Headspace" apps and try exercises from it often. Learn breathing and relaxation techniques.

- When it comes to eating out as a family, do not always take counsel from your children. Occasionally go to dinner where you and your spouse would like to go. In fact, if your children are old enough, leave them home with some macaroni and cheese or a "bake-it-yourself-cardboard pizza." Then, the next time you go out to eat as a family, they may be much more grateful.

- Plan a husband/wife vacation to your favorite spot every year.

- Take a class or a workshop on something you deeply desire to learn.

- Do a craft or make something creative.

- Declutter your room or office. Clean out your garage and get rid of all of things you have not used for ten years.

- Sing aloud in the shower or in your car. Starting the day

off with singing can put you in a stellar mood! I recommend getting a blue tooth speaker in your shower for this very reason. They are relatively cheap.

- Dance *like* no one is watching. Better yet, dance *when* no one is watching.

- Hike up in the mountains or in the woods near your home.

- Take a nap in a hammock in your back yard. Heck, take a nap anywhere.

- Listen to your favorite comedian and laugh hysterically. I recommend that everyone have a favorite comedian to listen to often.

- Exercise with no time limit. Do some good stretching while you listen to music.

- Float in a pool with awesome music playing in the background.

- Sleep in occasionally—as long as you would like!

- Go for a long walk with your spouse or one of your children.

- Watch a movie by the fireplace with some perfect snacks.

- Read a book by the pool. If you do not have a pool, read a book by someone else's pool.

- Listen to good music throughout the day and use music in your home to create a fun atmosphere. I remember dancing with our children to good music when they were younger—while we did our chores. The music helped tremendously!

In one of my happiest places on the earth—sitting with Janie, reading, and enjoying the beach on Hawaii's North Shore.

 *Why Mark stinks at self-nurturing*

SELF-SUFFICIENCY

"Those [parents] who do too much for their children will soon find they can do nothing with their children. So many children have been so much done for they are almost done in."
~ *Elder Neal A. Maxwell[80]*

Several years ago, I became aware of a family that would not allow their children to enter into the kitchen without parental permission. Regardless of how old you were, if you wanted a drink or a snack, you had to ask the mother for permission. I thought that sounded a bit odd and controlling. I learned later that it was the mother's way of keeping order in the kitchen. However, that sounded about as bizarre to me as a father who would not allow his children to play in the yard for fear that they would mess it up.

Not long after that, I was sitting in my living room, talking to a couple of my children, when I heard a loud noise coming from the kitchen. I turned around and noticed my two-year old daughter sliding a barstool across the kitchen floor (that was the source of the noise) towards the cupboards. Instead of saying anything, I sat quietly and watched what would happen next. The daughter climbed the barstool, stood on top of the counter, and then grabbed a cup from the cupboard. She then climbed down from her lofty perch, walked across the kitchen, went over to the refrigerator, and got herself a glass of ice water. As she began to drink, I silently rejoiced at her independence. I was thankful that someone so young had figured out how to do something on their own, without the help of their parents. That toddler became the same daughter, that, as a teen, woke herself up each morning, did her work without being asked, exercised as if she was training for the Olympics, and did her homework on her own. Today, she is teaching her children to follow the same pattern. The goal of parents should be to teach their children to become independent. One way to do that is to teach them specific life skills.

Suggestions:

- The goal of every parent should be to teach their children to become self-sufficient and self-sustaining. I assume that most of us do not want our adult children living in our basements, unemployed at age 35, playing video games all day and eating our food. However, many helicopter and coddling parents do not teach their children how to become self-sufficient and then wonder, years later, why their 40-year-old child still lives in their home and cannot hold a job. We have to prepare our children for the "real world," beginning at young ages!

- Give your children hard things to do. I remember when I was somewhere between 8-10 years old, my parents frequently gave me money to travel to the grocery store on my bike to purchase something for them.

- Too many young couples get married today and have no clue how to perform some of the most basic life skills. Parents should always be preparing their children for adulthood. Begin teaching your children life skills early on.

- Children should have chores and responsibilities. If your children do not have chores, they will never develop some of the crucial skills they will need later in life. Chores teach your children to be responsible and self-reliant.[81]

- Teach your children how to create order in their lives—beginning with their rooms!

- Children should do their homework on their own, without a parent hovering over them. Let children be stewards of themselves.

- Teach your children, when they are at the appropriate age, how to cook. I recommend that they learn how to make at least two breakfast meals, two lunch meals, and two dinner meals.

- Teach your children how to pick up after themselves, keep their rooms clean, clean their bathrooms, and clean a kitchen.

- Teach your children how to do their own laundry, fold and iron their clothes, and put their newly cleaned clothing away.

- Teach your children how to clean a garage.

- Teach them how to sew a button on a shirt or blouse.

- Teach them how to change the oil in a car.

- Teach them how to change a light bulb.

- Teach them some basic plumbing and electrical skills, beginning with how to unclog a toilet and replace a lightbulb.

- Teach them how to grocery shop, live off a budget, and save money. Money management is an incredible skill for children to acquire early in their lives. Jackson Brown suggested, "Take your teenagers with you when you buy a car or expensive household item and let them learn from the experience."[82]

- Teach your children how to manage and allocate their time in order to maximize their productivity and opportunities.

- Teach them how to keep their checking account balanced.

- Teach them how to put gas in a car and change a flat tire.

- Teach them how to deal with failure, how to cope with difficult things, and how to develop grit.

- When children have problems, ask them, "So, what are you going to do to solve that?" When they are younger, give them some options or choices to resolve issues.

- Point out your children's strengths often. Let them know that you see them as capable, independent, strong, and talented. Help them identify their positive attributes. Let them know that you have confidence in them.

SERVICE

"Service is the virtue that distinguished the great of all times and which they will be remembered by...It is the dividing line which separates the two great groups in the world—those who help and those who hinder, those who lift and those who lean, those who contribute and those who consume."
~ *Bryant S. Hinckley*[83]

I have learned in my life that true happiness and fulfillment come from serving and helping other people. Yes, we can do many things for ourselves that bring fleeting happiness. However, lasting happiness comes from serving our fellowmen. Service to others can often be found in small acts, like taking your neighbor's garbage cans out to the street, finding a newspaper in the street and throwing it up to your neighbor's porch, or snow shoveling your neighbor's driveway or sidewalk. However, do not hog all of the fun. Share this great gift and legacy of service with your children. I remember, on many occasions, taking my children with me to help a neighbor move, to help a family member with yard work, or to serve those in our community.

A good friend of mine, Randal Wright, shared with me

an experience he had. He showed up in his neighborhood to help a neighbor load up their moving truck. Then, he noticed another family show up to also help with the process. This was not just a mom or dad with a grumpy teenager. This was a mom and dad and their seven children. Together, the family worked and laughed as they served their neighbors. Randal later said, "I promise—they will not lose any of those children." What many parents do not understand is that self-worth in children is greatly enhanced when they turn outward and put others before themselves.

One of my favorite things I enjoyed as a parent was watching my children do things for each other and love and serve each other. Occasionally, they reached out to those outside of their circle. I remember when our elementary school daughter, Madison, became good friends with a boy in her class who was confined to a wheelchair. She would push him around during recess at school and stayed close to him during their classes. Sometimes she would go over to his house after school to play, and other times—she had him over to our home. I have always been proud of my daughter for reaching out to others. Today she is the mother of three children, and I watch her continue to serve and help those around her.

Suggestions:

- Teach your children that serving and helping other people is one of the greatest acts they can engage in. In fact, a wise man named Gordon Hinckley, son of Bryant S. Hinckley who was quoted at the top of this page, once said, "It is selfishness which is the cause of most of our misery."[84]

- One of the greatest ways for children to learn the art of service is by watching their parents serve other people.

- Teach your children that true happiness comes from doing things for other people.

- Teach your children to sacrifice their own wants in needs in order to do something for someone else. This is one of the most significant ways to prepare for adulthood.

- Teach your children that by serving and helping others, they can often put our own problems in a proper perspective. Serving others helps us obtain happiness in this life.

- Teach your children the joy of anonymous service. It can be fun and exciting to do something for someone and have them never know who did it!

- Take your children with you when you bring meals to the neighbors. Enlist your children's help when you watch the neighbor's children. When doing yardwork or service for others, make sure your children are engaged with you.

- Teach your children to be in tune to the needs of others. Be watchful and observant so that you will know and be aware of when others are in need.

- Plan family activities and trips that include opportunities to serve others.

- Always be on the lookout for people who may need your family's help. Teach your children to look around for those who look like they can use some extra help or encouragement.

- Make service opportunities fun. When your family goes out and serves someone, make it a pleasant experience. Treats and eating out afterwards will always make service more fun.

- Never remind someone of the service or kindness you have rendered to them. In fact, when you serve others, enjoy the blessing of anonymity.

With a wonderful perspective of service, my daughter, Madison, continues to serve her family and those in her community. I love this girl's grit and tenacity.

SPORTS

"Sports don't build character; they reveal it."
~ Attributed to John Wooden[85]

I once heard a father say that he would never participate in a sport unless he could participate with his family. I thought that was wise counsel. I have enjoyed playing whiffle ball and kick-ball in the back yard with our children. Basketball in the drive-way has also been a staple at our home. Several years ago, we went on a badminton spree, which was also enjoyable. Whatever sport you enjoy, include your whole family in it.

I have heard some parents say that they would not let their children participate in sports because of the "competition" or the potential injuries they could incur. I feel just the opposite. I personally believe that children can learn more life lessons from participating in sports than just about any other endeavor. I never wanted to deprive my children of the "thrill of victory" or the "agony of defeat." Personally, I learned some of the most difficult life lessons in sports, and I am glad that my children were able to do the same. I believe the sports my children played helped develop their character almost more than anything else they did.

Suggestions:

- Learn to enjoy a good sporting event. Support your local college and/or professional teams by occasionally attending games and wearing their jerseys proudly.

- Participate in sports with your family. Play sports with your kids in your backyard and driveway. When your children are participating in sports, try to have your family in attendance to show their love and support.

- Understand that sports are great for children. Participation in sports helps children academically, builds their self-worth, encourages them to work hard and accomplish difficult tasks, learn leadership skills, and develop coping strategies. Above all, sports help children stay physically fit and active.

- It never hurts to make friends with someone who has season tickets to one of your favorite teams.

- When watching your children's sporting events, cheer loudly for every player on the team—not just your kid. Furthermore, while watching your children play their sport, do not be an obnoxious fan and embarrass your kid. No yelling at the referee, umpire, players, or other parents. If you cannot control yourself, do not go. Teach your child to be a good sport and to be a team player. As a parent, do the same.

- Praise your children as they participate. Build them up and focus on the good things they do.

- Some of the greatest experiences I ever had as a parent were watching my children compete in sports and give it their all.

- Use sports as a way to connect with your children. Find reasons to drive your child home after their games and have great talks and discussions. Find ways to encourage and inspire them. If you are able, volunteer to help coach their teams.

- Expose your children to as many sports as possible, including sports they can do for the rest of their lives, like running, pickle ball, tennis, racquetball, swimming, and golf. Provide your children with the resources they need to be successful and have positive experiences in the sports they play. Provide them with good equipment. Send them to camps.

- After your children participate in games, matches, or tournaments, draw life lessons from their experiences. Teach them principles and help them identify concepts from their experiences that will help them in other areas of life. Most often, there are more lessons to process from losing than winning.

*With my twin daughters, Madison and McKenzie, at their last intramu-
ral football game of their college career.*

TABLE ETIQUETTE

"Who needs a book of etiquette? Everyone does.... For we must
all learn the socially acceptable ways of living."
~ Amy Vanderbilt[86]

Several years ago, I was at a professional conference with some colleagues. After our presentations were over, we took some of our colleagues and their significant others to a nice restaurant. To our surprise, one of our colleagues, knowing that we were hosting and would be paying for the meal, went a little crazy on their order. In essence, since they decided to "swing for the fence." They ordered steak, chicken, and lobster. That colleague's sole order ended up costing more than my hotel room that night. It was a reminder that when someone else is paying for the meal, we should be reasonable and respectable.

Suggestions:

- Do not begin eating until everyone is served his or her food.

- Women and children should always be served first. When it comes to eating meals, men should be the last ones to serve themselves for meals. A true gentleman makes sure that everyone else's needs are met before their very own. I see too many men today filling their plates two feet high with food while practically running over women and children to be the first in line.

- Put your napkin on your lap.

- Do not talk with your mouth full.

- When eating dinner over at someone else's home, always volunteer to help with the dishes and clean up.

- During table conversation, do not interrupt others when they are speaking.

- If someone invites you to lunch or dinner, you could assume that they are paying for you. Nevertheless, always offer to pay for yourself and the person with whom you are eating.

- If at a meal that someone else is paying for, do not order the most expensive thing on the menu, and do not overeat.

TEACHING YOUTH TO LEAD

"We constantly need to replenish the world's coterie of leaders. The current leaders move on, move up, or die off, yet the world's problems continue to grow. Where do we turn, then, if we have no new generation of leaders ready to step up to the challenges of our world?"
~ Pat Williams[87]

Several years ago, we lived in a new community. One of our friends was moving from one subdivision to another about two miles away. We were able to round up some men in the neighborhood to help this particular neighbor with his move. That Saturday, most of the dads brought their sons with them to help. Most of our sons that day were between the ages of 11 to 14. For some reason, one of the youngest boys there decided that he was in charge of the entire operation. He began bossing the adults and boys around as if he owned the place. Unfortunately for this bossy kid, no one really took him seriously or paid much attention to him. Everyone just ignored him and followed the directions from the man who was actually moving—since it was his stuff.

It was a reminder that no one really wants to follow dictator or a person who is not qualified to lead. People want to follow leaders who are competent. That young boy had never moved anything in his life—why would we follow someone who did not have a clue? Happily, we did not have to! Teach your children that true leaders are those who serve and help build others.

A true leader is really a servant to those they lead. They do not put themselves above anyone else. They are down to earth and do not mind getting dirty and grimy with the men and women they serve with. As pointed out by Dr. Hugh Nibley, these leaders have "a passion for *equality*. We think of great generals from David and Alexander on down, sharing their beans or *maza* with their men, calling them by their first names, marching along with them in the heat, sleeping on the ground, and being the first over the wall."[88]

Suggestions:

- To help your children become leaders, instill in them confidence. Let them know that you believe in them. Point out to them why they are good leaders. Give them responsibility and help them be successful in carrying out their responsibilities!

- Teach your children that in order to be leaders, they must show up and be prepared. Showing up is not enough—they need to be ready. I have associated with many youth leaders over the years who are good at part one; they show up. However, they often fail at part two; they are not prepared! These youth show up to meetings without paper, pencil, or plans. Teach them to be prepared when they show up.

- Teach your children to be bold enough to speak up. Most often, we need to hear more from the quiet youth—not just the loudest ones.

- Teach your children to learn to think outside of the box and be creative. There are often many ways to accomplish a task.

- Teach your children that leaders have to have a vision. They need to be leading their people somewhere. Leaders have to know where they are going and how to get their people there.

- Teach your children that leaders have to lead by example. They can never ask someone to do something that they are not doing themselves.

- Teach your children that good leaders unify and fortify those they are leading. They know how to build a team.

- Teach your children that great leaders do not care who gets the credit.

- Teach your children that leaders have to be organized. No one wants to follow a leader who lives in shambles.

- Teach your children to be problem solvers. Every group has a strong contingency of whiners and complainers. Instead of whining and complaining, teach them to solve problems. Most leaders do not need any more problems—they have plenty of problems. They need people to come to them with solutions.

- Teach your children that it will be difficult to lead if they do not have "people skills." They need to learn to be kind, friendly, polite, and caring. Few people respond to leaders who *do not* care about them. Great leaders love the people they serve.

- Teach your children that leaders will always have critics. Wherever there is a great leader, there will always be a loud critic nearby.

- Teach your children that leaders are not to do what is popular; they are to do what is right.

- Likewise, help your children learn to communicate positively and clearly. Teach them to be optimistic. A leader who is discouraged, depressed, and defeated is no longer a leader.

- Teach your children that a great leader must first be a great listener. Too many leaders like to flap their gums, but they are not listening to the people they should be serving.

- Teach your children that great leaders maintain a healthy sense of humor. Often, good humor can deescalate tense situations and make everyone in the room feel at ease.

- Teach your children that in order to be good leaders, they must be passionate about the cause they are leading. It will be difficult to lead troops into a battle with a casual, uncommitted leader.

THE FIVE-MINUTE DIFFERENCE

"What's the most important thing I can do today
that would make tomorrow better?"
~Rory Vaden[89]

Isn't it amazing what a difference that five minutes can make? If individuals would just take five minutes to invest in a task, it could positively affect so many things that surround them. It could affect the rest of their day, and in some cases, the rest of their week.

Many years ago, Janie and I purchased our first home. Almost immediately, we began some minor remodeling and home repairs. In those early days as homeowners, we did a significant amount of painting. Until then, I never understood that sometimes it took longer to prepare a room to paint than it did to actually paint it. As many people understand, in order to prepare the room for painting, we had to remove every electrical outlet cover and light switch cover. We also had to remove each piece of hardware from the doors. Then, we taped around everything that we did not want to paint, such as the trim, molding, and windows. It was a laborious process to say the least. Many times, it seemed it took a couple of hours to prepare a room and only an hour to actually paint with a roller.

Since I am an impatient person, I was becoming frustrated with how long it was taking to "prep" our hallway for painting. Instead of placing a drop cloth over the floor, I decided to paint without one. I did not want to waste any more time "prepping." I justified in my mind that I was a good painter and that I was probably not going to spill any paint on our ceramic tile floor anyway. Unfortunately, I was painting with a roller, where the paint tends to spray out everywhere. I stayed up late on a Saturday night painting the entire hallway and did not realize the seriousness of my mistake until the next morning. When I woke up, I inspected my incredible paint job and decided that everything looked wonderful. It was Janie who pointed out to me that there were white paint spots all over the tan colored ceramic tile. When I examined the floor closely, I realized that there were white paint spots everywhere—all over the tile, and in many cases, in the dark-brown-colored grout.

If only I would have taken an extra five minutes to lay down some drop clothes, I could have saved the hours it took me to scrape the paint off the tile and the grout. Even if I did not lay down drop clothes, if I would have noticed the paint drops immediately after I had painted, I probably could have taken five minutes and wiped it all up with a damp rag. To scrape the dried paint off the tile was tedious and seemed to take hours. As I scraped, a statement kept ringing in my ears that originated from Benjamin Franklin: "An ounce of prevention is worth a pound of cure."[90] Thankfully, I have learned my lesson. Today,

I will only paint a wall if there is a drop cloth protecting the floor. I have also learned that the "five-minute" difference can change my life in many areas—not just painting.

Suggestions:

- Take five minutes to check the oil and other fluids in your car. Such "preventative" maintenance can prevent a multitude of problems.

- Take five minutes to wipe down your kitchen counters and table after a meal. This practice is much easier than trying to chisel fossilized bananas and dried juice off your countertops the next day.

- Take five minutes to put all of your tools back in your toolbox. It is not worth hunting for your tools for hours because you were too lazy to put them back in their proper place.

- Take five minutes to put your lawn equipment back into your garage or shed. I know a person who left his lawn mower outdoors all summer. Consequently, the sprinklers and rainstorms soaked his mower. By the end of the summer, he was baffled that his mower would not start. I am sure his gas tank was full of water.

- Take five extra minutes to wash the dishes in your sink before you go to bed. If you do not, you may spend the next few days trying to peel dried spaghetti off your dishes. In fact, you may need a jackhammer to remove some of that sauce.

- In one case, if I would have just taken five minutes to fill up my car with gas, I wouldn't have had to spend two hours a little later walking to a gas station.

- Take five minutes to brush your teeth after every meal, and then you will not have to spend hours in the dental office—receiving thousands of dollars' worth of dental work.

- If you take five minutes to fold your clothes, you can avoid a week of wrinkles.

- If you take five minutes to fill the console of your car with snacks, you can avoid spending tons of cash going through the drive-through at the local fast food establishment when your children are on the verge of dying of hunger.

- If you take five minutes to clean the garbage and mess out of your car, it will look nice and clean each time you climb into your car to drive somewhere.

- If you take five minutes or more to fold the laundry and put it away, you will not have to spend 30 minutes sorting through a pile a clothes to find your kids missing sock.

- If you take five minutes to "spray-and-wash" a stain out of your shirt, you can avoid the inconvenience of having to throw your shirt away a few days later because you did not tend to that stain.

- If you take five minutes to put a bib on your baby or toddler before they eat, their clothes will last much longer.

- If you take five minutes to hang up your car keys in their appropriate place each time you walk into your home, you will not have to spend an hour looking for them later.

- Speaking of keys, if you took five minutes, or a little more, to get an extra set of keys made for your car and your home, you could avoid some major heartbreak and delays that are sure to come when you lose your keys.

- Or, to take the car key advice even further, if you take five minutes to put a "tile" on your keychain, when you lose your keys, you can find them using your "tile" phone app.

- If you take five minutes to rinse out your blender, you can avoid spending an hour trying to scrape off dried strawberries from the blender jar.

- Take five minutes each evening to straighten up and clean up your home before bedtime, and then you can awaken to a nice home each morning. I know some people who never do this. Consequently, over time, their house looks like it was hit by a hurricane. Then they end up spending hours, if not days, digging themselves out of the mess the have created.

- If you would take five minutes to clean out your car every time you come home, you could avoid spending half a Saturday, digging through your car to find your child's missing retainer case.

- Take five minutes to set up online bill pay with your bank, and avoid hours of paying bills in the future.

- Take five minutes each evening preparing yourself for the

next day. This includes getting your clothes ready, packing lunches, and laying out some of the things you may need for work, school, or other activities. This idea certainly beats the alternative of scrambling each morning like a lunatic trying to get out the door in time for your appointment.

• If you would take five extra minutes to order a second pair of prescription glasses, when you break or lose your glasses, you wouldn't have to walk around town squinting to see who is standing in front of you.

A story of "The Five-Minute Difference"

TIME MANAGEMENT

"Time flies on wings of lightening;
We cannot call it back.
It comes, then passes forward
Along its onward track.
And if we are not mindful,
The chance will fade away,
For life is quick in passing.
'Tis as a single day."
~Robert B. Baird[91]

We have all had issues with time—either being late, wasting time, procrastinating, or simply feeling like we never have enough! There have been many times in my life when I have felt completely overwhelmed—when I have simply had too many things for one person to do. However, instead of fretting or going into a paralysis where I simply froze, I learned that going to bed a little earlier and getting up early has allowed me to accomplish more than I should have been able too.

While in graduate school, I also worked full-time. At the

same time, I was married, and we had small children. I came to realize that the only way I could manage life was literally "one day at a time." I could not think of what needed to be done at the end of the week, or what projects had to be completed by the end of the month. All I could think about was what I had to do that day—and life became more manageable. On Mondays, I focused on what I had to do on Monday—and I did not worry about Tuesday until…. well, Tuesday. That perspective has allowed me to balance an extremely busy schedule.

Suggestions:

- Do a time audit and determine where you spend most of your time and where your time is often wasted.

- One of the secrets to success in life is to wake up at 5:00 a.m., or perhaps even earlier. It is amazing what you can accomplish when you wake up that early. When I engage in that program, I can often read scriptures, plan my day, exercise, read a book or even the newspaper, all before 8:00 a.m.

- Every morning, make a list of all of the things you have to accomplish. Then, work on your calendar, and determine where you can place your events and tasks. Make sure you prioritize your most urgent and important tasks. Other tasks may have to wait for another day.

- Because I believe we are on this earth to act and not be acted up, I recommend that you plan every month, every week, and every day of your life. Fill your calendar with meaningful activities that will bring joy and happiness.

- Do not confuse activity with accomplishment.

- When planning your days, always consider your goals and how you can build them into your schedule.

- Plan each day and execute!

- You must be intentional about the time you spend with your family. Put those moments each day on your calendar and make them happen! Schedule and plan important events with your spouse, children, and friends.

- Plan times for rest and recreation.

- Keep your calendar in front of you so that you can stay on task throughout the day. Use technology to help you stay focused and accountable.

- Focus on completing one task at a time. Sometimes you may find it necessary to place a time limit on each task.

- Take breaks between tasks. You have earned it.

- Get organized!

- Remove things from your calendar that are not essential. You may have to learn to say "no" to others. You have to have boundaries. You cannot do everything!

- Do not become so regimented with your calendar that you cannot be flexible.

- Make sure you have your priorities in the right order. No one ever said on his or her deathbed, "I sure wish I would have spent more time at the office." Instead, most people regret towards the end of their lives that they did not spend enough time with those whom they love the very most.

 *A story about time management*

TRADITIONS

"Build traditions in your families that will bring
you together, for they can demonstrate your devotion,
love, and support for one another."
~ L. Tom Perry[92]

Although there are many traditions that I could mention, there is one that was a bit unusual, but memorable. My son, Brandon, was one of the outstanding players on his high school football team. Not surprisingly, he went on to have a stellar career in college. Nevertheless, in high school, we had a tradition that I will always remember. After each Friday Night Football game, I would drive over to the field house where I would patiently wait for my son. Eventually, he would come out of the fieldhouse and get into my car. His tradition was that he was always the last one out. We would talk about the game in vivid detail as we drove to the *Wendy's* drive-through.

We would load up on Frosties, hamburgers, and fries, and then head home and continue eating and talking about the game. Often, by that time, High School Highlights for all of the games in the Dallas Area were being aired on one of the local television stations. We would watch some of those highlights, then I would go off to bed, and my son would go out with his friends. It was a great father-and-son connecting time. Traditions are what bind families together. Consistency is what gives a tradition efficacy.

Suggestions:

- Ask your children what your family traditions are. How they respond could be insightful!

- Occasionally set up a tent and camp out in your backyard.

- Make sure you reserve one night a week for family fun and activities.

- Consider a tradition of eating regularly at a certain restaurant. For a time, we had a family tradition of eating at a favorite restaurant on the first evening of the school year.

- Establish bedtime traditions with your children when they are young that include eating a snack, brushing their teeth, getting dressed in their PJs, and having story time. There should be a story every night!

- Have a regular family movie night, complete with popcorn and other snacks.

- Have a favorite family game.

- Create a tradition of serving and helping other people.

- Go for family walks or bike rides.

- Teach your children about their heritage often. Tell them stories of your ancestors.

- Take your children out to eat at their favorite restaurant after their performances, games, and other events. Often, on trips, we would stop at some of the exact same places to eat every time. Our children always knew that Amarillo, Texas meant *Rudy's Barbeque*, and St. George Utah always meant *The Pizza Factory*.

- Have a family expression or a family motto that can be repeated often. One of ours was, "Always be where you are supposed to be, when you are supposed to be there, doing what you are supposed to be doing." Other expressions could be, "Be on time," or, "Be a leader—not a follower." I know one family that had coined the expression, "No empty chairs." This meant, when we get to heaven, we want all of you to be there!

- Consider the tradition that when a family member has an important activity, that the entire family comes out to support them.

- A wonderful tradition is for parents to spend one-on-one time with each of their children each month. Some parents do this by taking their children out to eat, or to do a fun activity. I know a father who had four children. Each week of the month, he would take one of his children out to breakfast. In those settings, he learned to be a great listener, and he devoted his full attention to his children.

- Family trips and campouts can become wonderful and memorable traditions.

- Establish spiritual traditions in your home to teach your

children values and to deepen their faith. These traditions include family prayer, family scripture study, attending worship services together, talking about the gospel in your home, having gospel discussions while you work together or drive in the car, listening to spiritual messages while driving on family trips, watching movies together with religious content, etc.

- Many traditions can center on food. Growing up, we all knew that Sunday night was steak night and Friday night was pizza night. Saturday mornings were pancakes and waffles.

- Watch movies on the family trampoline and fall asleep.

- Sing and dance together while you do the dishes and clean the kitchen.

- Go on Sunday walks together.

- Make crazy family videos together.

- Take a photograph of each of your children in the same place each year on the first day of school. Take a family photograph every year.

- Eat one family meal together each day around the kitchen table.

- Ensure that your holidays are full of traditions.

- Plan a summer vacation each year—as a family.

I have always believed that a family that plays together, stays together.

A story about traditions

WORK

Several years ago, Janie and I were driving home from running some errands. As we begin to drive down our street, I noticed my college-aged son and his friend walking through our neighborhood. They both were loaded down with equipment and supplies. We stopped, rolled down the window, and asked them what they were doing. My son explained that they were knocking on neighbor's doors, trying to drum up customers and jobs for their window washing business they had just created. My son and his friend were both recently married, and they also played college football. In fact, they had been at practice most of the day. Here they were at 7:00 in the evening, trying to make financial ends meet. As I drove away, looking at my son and his friend through the rear-view mirror of my car, I thought to myself, "I'll probably never have to worry about him providing for his family. If his work ethic is this solid, he's going to do just fine in life." He has proven that belief to be true. My son is one of the hardest workers I know.

Suggestions:

- One of the most important traits that parents can pass down to their children is a work ethic. With the ability to work—and work hard—your children will be able to achieve the impossible. A respected religious leader wrote, "If children are raised with a poor attitude about work and do not learn to sustain themselves, they will be weak and dependent as adults. They may ultimately become a liability to society instead of making a real contribution."[94]

- Strive to be known in your neighborhood and community as the family with hard-working children. People in our communities have hired our children because they knew of their work ethic.

- Teach children at a young age the value of work. Teach them the joy of an honest labor and the satisfaction that can come from seeing a job accomplished.

- Teach your children that work is good therapy for most problems and the antidote for worry and fear.

- Share with your children some of your experiences with "hard work." Pass down those lessons to the next generation.

- Teach your children that knowing how to work in life will give them an advantage over most of their peers. There are many intelligent people in the world, but there are very few who know how to work hard. The prizes do not often go to the intelligent—they go to those who work the hardest.

- Work alongside your children. Do not expect them to know how to clean their room when they are two years old. They will need to be taught! Work together as a team.

- Even though having your children work with you will slow you down, resist the temptation to work alone. So what if you have to re-mow the front yard—your child is learning the joy of work!

- While working together, engage in meaningful conversations, share humorous stories and experiences and share life's lessons together.

- Since most of us do not live on farms, the challenge often becomes finding meaningful work for our children to do. In reality, there are plenty for them to do. They can work in the yard, do chores in the home, clean up garbage in the neighborhood, do service for a neighbor, volunteer at a hospital, learn to make meals, shovel snow, and even deliver newspapers. Even reading can be a meaningful work activity—especially if they are learning a skill!

- Make sure that your children have a regular list of chores to do. Teach them that work comes before play.

- Children can be engaged in family work projects, such as home improvements. Teach your children to paint, hang sheetrock, build fence, tile floors, and fix basic plumbing and electrical problems.

- Ensure that your teenagers find part-time work and summer employment.

- If you own a business, be aware of the challenges that could come as your hire your children work for you. Although that is a popular practice, understand that children will learn much more if they work for someone else besides their parents.

- Consider creating a "side business" with your family where you all can work together as a team.

- Create a culture and tradition in your family. Be known in your community as a family who knows how to work hard.

Left, my grandson Luke mowing his lawn, and on the right, my youngest daughter, Natalie, who once made herself lemonade while she watched her sisters do some yard work. Yikes!

YARD WORK

"If you have a garden and a library,
you have everything you need."
~ Marcus Tullius Cicero[95]

As a professional educator, I rarely am able to see the fruit of my labors. If I have affected a student in a positive way, I rarely hear about those occasions. Perhaps at the end of every semester, a handful of students will express their thanks, or they will share with me how my class has helped them. However, most days of my professional life, I teach several classes, meet with several students, attend a committee meeting, and work on some research or writing projects. At the end of each day, I have little evidence of what good I have done.

And that, my friends, is where my lawn comes in. I can put my headphones on, dial up some awesome country music on Pandora, and begin mowing my lawn. I can escape into my fantasy world as I mow, effortlessly, back and forth. After edging, trimming, and mowing, I can stand on my street and view the front of my house and say to myself, "That yard looks spectacular." The fruits of my labor in the yard are noticeable, tangible, and immediately obvious. I can almost obtain more satisfaction from one day of yard work than from an entire semester of teaching hundreds of students. Taking care of my lawn is one of the greatest forms of therapy for my soul.

Suggestions:

- Try to have a nice-looking yard with a strong sense of curb appeal. Keep your lawn clean; pick up garbage, toys, bikes, and other clutter from your yard daily. Try to make your yard "green and clean."

- If your climate allows for it, always plant several fruit trees. In fact, I like the idea of planting a tree in your yard for each of your children. Some suggest planting a tree each year—on someone's birthday.

- Have a spot somewhere in your yard to grow a nice vegetable garden each year. Have your children help you plant the garden and water it often.

- There are several things you will need to make your lawn green and clean. First, you will want a sprinkler system. Second, you should weed and fertilize regularly. I like throwing some steer manure on my lawn every spring. Third, consider mowing your lawn diagonally. This will give your lawn amazing curb appeal.

- Experts recommend watering your lawn in the morning rather than the evening. Never water in the middle of the day. The water will evaporate before it gets down into the roots.

- Aerate your lawn once a year.

- Keep your mower blade sharp and cut your grass higher rather than lower.

 *The importance of work ethic*

 *Lessons from yard work*

CONCLUSION

As you have read these suggestions, you may have thought that they are insightful or perhaps even revelatory. You may also have thought, "All of these ideas are just common sense. Why would you need a book full of common-sense suggestions?" I agree. I think most of life's challenges can be resolved with some good, ole'-fashioned common sense. Here is the problem: from my observation, most people can solve most of life's problems with common sense—except sometimes the challenges in their own family.

Let me give you an example. For years as a marriage and family therapist, I have met with individuals and families with some notoriety—CEOs of corporations, presidents of organizations, church leaders, civic leaders, and even government leaders. These people are paid large sums of money to solve problems every day. That is what they do! However, what has been amazing to me is to watch these same individuals struggle with solving the problems in their families. Yes, literally CEOs not wanting, or not even teaching, their children to work. Presidents of parent-teacher organizations who do not require their children to do homework or even live by a schedule. Millionaires who have never taught their children how to manage money. High school coaches who have children who have never played a sport. Doctors whose children are morbidly obese and addicted to video games. I could go on for pages. I do not want to come across as hypocritical. I will confess that I, one who has studied marriage and family topics for years and who has written several books on the topic, have made some stupid parenting mistakes as well! My wife would tell you that my mistakes are not limited to parenting but also trickle into the marriage. Okay, maybe somedays "pour" into the marriage.

And that's the point: no one is immune to trouble and challenge. We are all in this together. We are all in this together. Most of us need all of the help we can get. If this book of advice and suggestions can help one person, then I will sleep very peacefully tonight. Others may read this book and think, "Heck, I could write this book. In fact, I could write one better!" I am sure you can! Please do, I would love to read it. I need all of the help I can get!

I invite you to keep on trying, keep loving, and never give up on members of your family. This is a wonderful life—we just need to seize those special moments that come each day and make them all count! The time we have with our children is relatively short. Consider that when our children are born, we have 6,570 days left with them until they turn 18 and leave home. By the time they turn eight, we only have 3,650 days left. By the time they are twelve and entering into middle school, it is amazing to consider that we only have 2,190 days left with them. By the time they are sixteen and ready to drive, we only have 730 days left. It does not matter how much money we have, who we are related to, or how significant we view ourselves; there is nothing that we can do to get those days back. We must savor every moment we have with our children because, all too soon, they will leave our homes and begin to build their own lives.

Treasure the moments you have together, make memories together, laugh together, and cry together. There is no greater blessing in this world than to be part of a loving family, a loving community, and to have great friends

With love,

Mark

REFERENCES

[1] LDS Church News, 9 July 2015.

[2] Samuel Johnson, The International Dictionary of Thoughts, complied by J.P. Bradley, Leo F. Daniels, Thomas C. Jones, [Chicago, Illinois: J.G. Ferguson Publishing Company, 1969], 356

[3] Jackson Brown, Jr., The Complete Life's Little Instruction Book, [Nashville, Tenn., Thomas Nelson Publishers, 1997], 1035.

[4] https://www.huffingtonpost.com.au/2017/10/18/weve-broken-down-your-entire-life-into-years-spent-doing-tasks_a_23248153/

[5] President Spencer W. Kimball, "Home: The Place to Save Society," Ensign, January 1975.

[6] President John F. Kennedy, State of the Union Message, U.S. News and World Report, 22 January 1962, 90.

[7] Brigham Young, The Teachings of President Brigham Young, Vol. 3 1852-1854, ed. Fred C. Collier [Salt Lake City, Utah: Collier's Publishing Co., 1987], 8.

[8] Jackson Brown, Jr., The Complete Life's Little Instruction Book, [Nashville, Tenn., Thomas Nelson Publishers, 1997], 1304.

[9] Robert Frost, "Mending Wall," Poetry Foundation, accessed 18 October 18, 2021; https://www.poetryfoundation.org/poems/44266/mending-wall

[10] H. Wallace Goddard, The Frightful and Joyous Journey of Family Life: Applying Gospel Insights in the Home, [Salt Lake City: Bookcraft, 1997], 96-97

[11] Dave Ramsey, as cited in "How we found $6,000 by cutting everyday expenses," in What the FI: Figuring Out Financial Independence,

accessed 18 October 2021; https://whatthefi.com/how-we-found-6000-by-cutting-everyday-expenses/

[12] Mark Sullivan, The International Dictionary of Thoughts, complied by J.P. Bradley, Leo F. Daniels, Thomas C. Jones, [Chicago, Illinois: J.G. Ferguson Publishing Company, 1969], 112.

[13] David O. McKay, Conference Report, April 1935, 116, as cited by J.E. McCullough, Home: The Savior of Civilization, (1924), 42.

[14] Know Your Quotes, accessed 18 October 2021; https://www.knowyourquotes.com/If-You-Think-Nobody-Cares-If-You39re-Alive-Try-Missing-A-Couple-Of-Car-Payments-Earl-Wilson.html

[15] Jose A. Teixeira, "Seeking the Lord," Ensign, May 2015.

[16] Gordon B. Hinckley, Standing For Something, 47.

[17] Bill Vaughan, in Dr. Laurence J. Peter, Peter's Quotations: Ideas for Our Time, [New York: William Morrow and Company, Inc., 1977], 118.

[18] 1937 September, Reader's Digest, Volume 31, (Freestanding quotation), 99, The Reader's Digest Association.

[19] Jackson Brown, Jr., The Complete Life's Little Instruction Book, [Nashville, Tenn., Thomas Nelson Publishers, 1997], 1245.

[20] Mother Teresa, Good Reads, accessed 25 September 2021; https://www.goodreads.com/quotes/49502-i-alone-cannot-change-the-world-but-i-can-cast

[21] Bill Gates, BrianyQuote, accessed 17 August 2021; https://www.brainyquote.com/quotes/bill_gates_173261

[22] Thomas J. Stanley and William D. Danko, The Millionaire Next Door: The Surprising Secrets of American's Wealthy, [New York: Taylor Trade Publishing, 2010], 208.

[23] H. Wallace Goddard, The Frightful and Joyous Journey of Family Life: Applying Gospel Insights in the Home, [Salt Lake City: Bookcraft, 1997], 77-78.

[24] C.S. Lewis, GoodReads, accessed 21 September 2021; https://www.goodreads.com/quotes/790437-take-care-it-is-so-easy-to-break-eggs-without

[25] Jackson Brown, Jr., The Complete Life's Little Instruction Book, [Nashville, Tenn., Thomas Nelson Publishers, 1997], 166.

[26] Personal notes of the author. 25 August 2009.

[27] Dr. Madeline Levine, The Price of Privilege, [New York: Harper Collins Publishers, 2006], 76.

[28] Dr. Richard S. Taylor, The Disciplined Life: The Mark of Christian Maturity, [Minneapolis, Minnesota: Bethany House Publishers, 1962], 27-28.

[29] Message Monday, 16 November 2016, Leave Sooner, Drive Slower, Live Longer, Transportation Matters for Iowa, accessed 15 August 2021; https://www.transportationmatters.iowadot.gov/2015/11/message-monday-nov-16-2015-leave-sooner-drive-slower-live-longer.html

[30] Robert E. Lee, in Dr. Laurence J. Peter, Peter's Quotations: Ideas for Our Time, [New York: William Morrow and Company, Inc., 1977], 175.

[31] John Bartlett, Bartlett's Familiar Quotations, 18th Edition, [New York: Little, Brown, and Company, 2012], 158:n7

[32] Henry Van Dyke, The International Dictionary of Thoughts, complied by J.P. Bradley, Leo F. Daniels, Thomas C. Jones, [Chicago, Illinois: J.G. Ferguson Publishing Company, 1969], 365.

[33] Samuel Johnson, The International Dictionary of Thoughts, complied by J.P. Bradley, Leo F. Daniels, Thomas C. Jones, [Chicago, Illinois: J.G. Ferguson Publishing Company, 1969], 356.

[34] Og Mandino, Quotefancy, accessed 18 April 2021; https://quotefancy.com/quote/878590/Og-Mandino-The-greatest-legacy-we-can-leave-our-children-is-happy-memories

[35] Adrian Gostick, "More Smiles Per Gallon: Ten Ways to Make Family Vacations more Fun," Ensign, June 1991.

[36] Liat Collins, The Jerusalem Post; as cited by Rabbi Harold S. Kushner, Conquering Fear: Living Boldly in an Uncertain World, [New York: Anchor Books, 2010], 5.

[37] Jackson Brown, Jr., The Complete Life's Little Instruction Book, [Nashville, Tenn., Thomas Nelson Publishers, 1997], 783.

[38] Dennis Prager, Happiness is a Serious Problem, [New York: Harper Collins, 1998], 59.

[39] Dave Ramsey, The Total Money Makeover: A Proven Plan for Financial Fitness, [Nashville, Tennessee: Nelson Books, 2003], 19.

[40] Jackson Brown, Jr., The Complete Life's Little Instruction Book, [Nashville, Tenn., Thomas Nelson Publishers, 1997], 91.

[41] Ezra Taft Benson, God, Family, Country, [Salt Lake City, Utah: Deseret Book, 1974], 241.

[42] Dorothy Parker, in Laurence J. Peter, comp., Peter's Quotations, (New York: William Morrow and Co., 1977), 77.

[43] Dr. Randal A. Wright, A Case for Chastity [USA: National Family Institute, 1993], 42.

[44] Max Lucado, Anxious for Nothing: Finding Calm in a Chaotic World, [Thomas Nelson: Nashville, Tenn, 2017], 96.

[45] Jackson Brown, Jr., The Complete Life's Little Instruction Book, [Nashville, Tenn., Thomas Nelson Publishers, 1997], 383.

[46] Dr. Madeline Levine, The Price of Privilege, [New York: Harper Collins Publishers, 2006], 76.

[47] Daniel Coyle, The Little Book of Talent: 52 Tips for Improving Your Skills, [New York: Bantam Books, 2012], 110.

[48] Neal A. Maxwell, The Neal A. Maxwell Quote Book, edited by Cory H. Maxwell, (Salt Lake City: Bookcraft, 1997), 152.

[49] 100+ Best Christmas Quotes: Funny, Family, Inspirational, and More, Homemade Gifts Made Easy; accessed 7 July 2021; https://www.homemade-gifts-made-easy.com/christmas-quotes.html

[50] Jackson Brown, Jr., The Complete Life's Little Instruction Book, [Nashville, Tenn., Thomas Nelson Publishers, 1997], 673.

[51] Funnytweeter.com; accessed 7 July 2021; https://funnytweeter.com/no-trip-to-home-depot-is-complete-without-at-least-two-more-trips-to-home-depot-for-what-you-didnt-know-you-needed-to-buy-the-first-time/

[52] Alexander Pope, The International Dictionary of Thoughts, complied

by J.P. Bradley, Leo F. Daniels, Thomas C. Jones, [Chicago, Illinois: J.G. Ferguson Publishing Company, 1969], 366.

[53] John Ruskin, The International Dictionary of Thoughts, complied by J.P. Bradley, Leo F. Daniels, Thomas C. Jones, [Chicago, Illinois: J.G. Ferguson Publishing Company, 1969], 371.

[54] George Barrell Cheever, The International Dictionary of Thoughts, complied by J.P. Bradley, Leo F. Daniels, Thomas C. Jones, [Chicago, Illinois: J.G. Ferguson Publishing Company, 1969], 372.

[55] Agnes Repplier, Quotes.Net, https://www.quotes.net/quote/8922, accessed November 8, 2021.

[56] Joseph B. Wirthlin, "The Virtue of Kindness," Ensign, May 2005.

[57] Adele Faber and Elaine Mazlish, Liberated Parents, Liberated Children [New York: Association Press, 1974].

[58] Dr. John Gottman and Nan Silver, Why Marriages Succeed or Fail… And How to Make Them Last, [New York: Simon and Schuster, 1994], 57.

[59] William G. Dyer and Phillip R. Kunz, "Keys to Developing Effective Families," Ensign, June 1989; https://www.churchofjesuschrist.org/study/ensign/1989/06/keys-to-developing-effective-families?lang=eng

[60] Padilla-Walker & Carlo, "Longitudinal Change in Adolescents' Prosocial Behavior Toward Strangers, Friends, and Family, Adolescence, November 2017.

[61] As cited in Stephen R. Covey, The 7 Habits of Highly Effective People, [New York: Simon & Schuster, 1989], 301.

[62] Henri Frederic Amiel, The International Dictionary of Thoughts, complied by J.P. Bradley, Leo F. Daniels, Thomas C. Jones, [Chicago, Illinois: J.G. Ferguson Publishing Company, 1969], 534.

[63] Benjamin Franklin, The International Dictionary of Thoughts, complied by J.P. Bradley, Leo F. Daniels, Thomas C. Jones, [Chicago, Illinois: J.G. Ferguson Publishing Company, 1969], 534.

[64] Julie Lythcott-Haims, How To Raise An Adult: Break Free of the Overparenting Trap and Prepare Your Kid for Success, (New York: Henry Holt and Company, 2015), 81.

[65] Some of these ideas come from, How to Raise An Adult, 81.

[66] A Dictionary of Thoughts: Being a Cyclopedia of Laconic Quotations from the Best Authors of the World, Both Ancient and Modern, ed. Tryon Edwards, [New York, New York: Cassell Publishing Company, 1891], 329.

[67] Elder Jeffrey R. Holland, "How Do I Love Thee?" Brigham Young University Speeches 1999-2000, 160-161.

[68] Charles J. Sykes, 50 Rules Kids Won't Learn in School: Real World Antidotes to Feel-Good Education, [New York: St. Martin's Press, 2007], 2.

[69] Fred Rogers, Quotefancy; accessed 18 October 2021; https://quotefancy.com/quote/807379/Fred-Rogers-I-ve-always-wanted-to-have-a-neighbor-just-like-you-I-ve-always-wanted-to

[70] Spencer W. Kimball, Ensign, May 1978, 5.

[71] Dr. Urie Brofenbrenner, "Nobody Home: The Erosion of the American Family," Psychology Today, May 1977.

[72] Brian K. Barber, Joseph E. Olsen, and Shobha C. Shagle, "Associations between Parental Psychological and Behavioral Control and Youth Internalized and Externalized Behaviors," Child Development, 65, 4, 1120-1136. https://doi.org/10.1111/j.1467-8624.1994.tb00807.x

[73] As cited in Michelle Watson, Dad, Here's What I Really Need from You: A Guide for Connecting with Your Daughter's Heart, [Eugene, Oregon: Harvest House Publishers, 2014], 77.

[74] Attributed to John Wesley, as cited in Hugh Stowell Brown, "Cleanliness is Next to Godliness," Lectures to the Men of Liverpool, [London: Partridge & Company, 1858], 3.

[75] Jackson Brown, Jr., The Complete Life's Little Instruction Book, [Nashville, Tenn., Thomas Nelson Publishers, 1997], 303.

[76] Dr. Madeline, The Price of Privilege, [New York: Harper Collins Publishers, 2006], 77.

[77] Hara Estroff Morano, A Nation of Wimps, [New York, New York: Crown Publishing Group, 2008], 262.

[78] The Best Self-Care Inspirational Quotes, Flourishing Over Fifty;

https://flourishingoverfifty.com/best-self-care-inspirational-quotes/

[79] Stephen R. Covey, The Seven Habits of Highly Effective People: 25th Anniversary Edition, [New York: Simon & Schuster, 2004], 299.

[80] Neal A. Maxwell, "The Man of Christ," Ensign, May 1975, 101.

[81] 10 Evidence-based Tips to Raising a Happy and Self-Reliant Kid; https://raising-independent-kids.com/10-scientifically-proven-tips-for-raising-self-reliant-responsible-and-happy-kids/

[82] Jackson Brown, Jr., The Complete Life's Little Instruction Book, [Nashville, Tenn., Thomas Nelson Publishers, 1997], 1122.

[83] Bryant S. Hinckley, quoted by Stephen R. Covey, First Things First, 306.

[84] Gordon B. Hinckley, Ensign, November 1988, 54.

[85] "Sports Do Not Build Character; They Reveal It," Quote Investigator; accessed 24 July 2021; https://quoteinvestigator.com/2015/04/08/sports/

[86] Amy Vanderbilt, The International Dictionary of Thoughts, complied by J.P. Bradley, Leo F. Daniels, Thomas C. Jones, [Chicago, Illinois: J.G. Ferguson Publishing Company, 1969], 263.

[87] Pat Williams, Coaching Your Kids to be Leaders, [New York: Warner Books, 2005], 9.

[88] Dr. Hugh Nibley, "Leaders and Managers," Brigham Young University Speeches, 19 August 1983; https://speeches.byu.edu/talks/hugh-nibley/leaders-managers/

[89] Mary Halton, "Multiply Your Time by Asking Four Questions About the Stuff on Your To-Do List," Ideas.Ted.Com, 28 January 2019; https://ideas.ted.com/multiply-your-time-by-asking-4-questions-about-the-stuff-on-your-to-do-list/

[90] Benjamin Franklin, Quotefancy, accessed 19 January 2022; https://quotefancy.com/quote/772108/Benjamin-Franklin-An-ounce-of-prevention-is-worth-a-pound-of-cure

[91] Robert B. Baird, "Improve the Shining Moments," Latter Day Saint Hymnbook, no. 226.

[92] L. Tom Perry, Ensign, May 1985, 23.

[93] Elder L. Tom Perry, "Train Up a Child," Ensign, November 1988, 74.

[94] Gene R. Cook, Raising Up a Family To the Lord, [Salt Lake City: Deseret Book, 1993], 226.

[95] Marcus Tullius Cicero, BrainyQuote, accessed 18 October 2021; https://www.brainyquote.com/quotes/marcus_tullius_cicero_104340

Made in the USA
Las Vegas, NV
19 March 2022

45949833R10160